Mastering Business Continuity

A Comprehensive Guide to ISO 22301 Implementation

Part: *Two*

MASTERING BUSINESS CONTINUITY

WORKSHOP BOOK — Part Two

A Comprehensive Guide to ISO 22301 Implementation

Understand & Implement ISO Standards

DR. MOHAMED-ALI IBRAHIM

ABOUT THE AUTHOR & INSTRUCTOR

DR. MOHAMED-ALI IBRAHIM

Top Skills

- Quality & Risk Management,
- Intercultural Skills,
- Management Consulting
- Master in Translation Studies
- Master in Interpretation
- Ph.D. in Quality & Risk Management

Languages

English, Arabic, German

Honors-Awards

- Austrian State Award
- International German Award
- SABRE International Award (PR Oscar)
- Best Practice Award, Vienna-Austria
- Top Expert 2021 and 2022 in Quality Management (Erfolg 2021 and 2022)

Publication

25 books (on Amazon) about Business Administration, Quality Management, and Translation Science.

The most important literature on the platform AMAZON

[Click Here](#)

Positions & Responsibilities:

Senior Lead Auditor and ME Director of Quality Austria (1998 - 2005), The Austrian Standards Institute (2006 - 2019), TÜV AUSTRIA (2005 - 2023), ATC (2022 - Now), UK, and I-LICS (International Localization Industry Certification System), Vienna, Austria (2011 - Now).

Dr. Mohamed-Ali Ibrahim is an accredited Lead Auditor for ISO 22301:2019 – Security

and resilience - Business continuity management systems - Requirements

He is also accredited as a Lead Auditor for the following Translation/Interpretation Standards

ISO 17100 for Translation Service Providers,

ISO 13611 for Community Interpreting,

and ISO 18587 for Machine Translation Post-editing

For further information, please visit: https://translationstandards.net/

„Plus 15 further ISO Standards in the Translation/Localization/MPE Industry. Dr. Ibrahim is also accredited for the following ISO Standards: ISO 9001, ISO 21001, ISO 29993, ISO 29991, ISO 29994, ISO 21989, ISO 20228, ISO 2603, ISO 24019, ISO 18841, ISO 21720, ISO 20771, ISO 22259, ISO 11669, ISO 23155)."

☐ The expertise includes Consultation, Training, and Certification.

☐ A former member of the Standards Committee at the Austrian Quality Authority and participated in developing the European Norm EN15038 for the field of translation which became the basis for ISO17100:2015

☐ Dr. Ibrahim acts now also as a "Senior Lead Auditor" for ATCC:

https://atccertification.com/meet-the-auditor-mohamed-ali-ibrahim/

☐ Conducted +750 different Quality Audits (Pre-Audits, Initial Audits, Surveillance Audits, and Recertification Audits) worldwide.

☐ Key-note speaker at international sector conferences. Trainer, Coach, Consultant, and Lead Auditor since 1998.

☐ Master in Translation Studies from Karl-Franzens University, Graz, Austria

☐ Master in Interpretation from Karl-Franzens University, Graz, Austria

☐ Ph.D. in Quality & Risk Management in healthcare institutions

TABLE OF CONTENTS

About The Author & Instructor 3
Introduction 7
Chapter 6: Resources for ISO 22301 Implementation 9
    6.1 Introduction 9
    6.2 Human Resources 12
    6.3 Technological Tools 16
    6.4 Financial Resources 19
    6.5 External Resources 22
    6.6 Time 26
    6.7 Infrastructure 29
    6.8 Summary 32

Chapter 7: Training, Awareness, and Competence in BCMS 35
    7.1 Introduction 35
    7.2 Building a Training Program for BCMS 37
    7.3 Cultivating Awareness about BCMS 40
    7.4 Developing Competence in BCMS 43
    7.5 Role of Leadership in BCMS Training and Awareness 45
    7.6 Evaluating BCMS Training and Competence Development 48
    7.7 Continual Improvement of BCMS Training and Competence 51
    7.8 Summary 54

Chapter 8: Internal Audit and Management Review 57
    8.1 Introduction 57
    8.2 The Role of Internal Audit in BCMS 58
    8.3 Audit Planning and Preparation 61
    8.4 Conducting the Internal Audit 63
    8.5 Post-Audit Activities 66
    8.6 Management Review of the BCMS 71
    8.7 Conducting the Management Review 74
    8.8 Continuous Improvement through Audit and Review 78
    8.9 Summary 81

Chapter 9: Maintaining and Improving the BCMS 84
    9.1 Introduction 84
    9.2 Continual Improvement in BCMS: An Overview 85
    9.3 Monitoring and Measuring the BCMS 87
    9.4 Performance Evaluation and Analysis 90

9.5 Addressing Non-conformities and Corrective Actions 93
9.6 Regular Review and Update of the BCMS 95
9.7 Role of Innovation in BCMS Improvement 98
9.8 Maintaining Readiness and Resilience 101
9.9 Summary 104

Chapter 10: External Audits and ISO 22301 Certification 107

10.1 Introduction 107
10.2 Preparing for an External Audit 108
10.3 The External Audit Process 111
10.4 ISO 22301 Certification Process 113
10.5 Post-Certification Activities 116
10.6 Surveillance and Recertification Audits 119
10.7 Managing Non-Conformities During External Audits 123
10.8 Leveraging ISO 22301 Certification for Business Advantage 126
10.9 Summary 128

INTRODUCTION

Advanced: Implementing ISO 22301 for Effective Business Continuity

Welcome to Part II of our comprehensive e-book on implementing ISO 22301 for effective business continuity management. In Part I, we laid the foundation by introducing you to the key concepts, principles, and benefits of ISO 22301. Now, in Part II, we delve deeper into the practical aspects of implementation, equipping you with the resources, strategies, and knowledge needed to successfully integrate the standard within your organization.

Chapter 6: Resources for ISO 22301 Implementation Implementing ISO 22301

requires a careful allocation of resources. In this chapter, we explore the various resources essential for a successful implementation, including human resources, technological tools, financial commitment, and the potential benefits of external consultancies. By understanding the necessary resources and how to effectively leverage them, you can set a solid foundation for the rest of your ISO 22301 journey.

Chapter 7: Training and Awareness Ensuring that your employees are well-trained

and aware of the significance of business continuity planning is crucial for the success of your Business Continuity Management System (BCMS). In this chapter, we guide you through the process of conducting effective training sessions and raising awareness about the importance of business continuity within your organization. By empowering your employees with the necessary knowledge, you can cultivate a culture of resilience and preparedness.

Chapter 8: Internal Auditing and Management Review Internal audits and

management reviews play a vital role in maintaining the effectiveness of your BCMS. In Chapter 8, we provide insights into conducting internal audits for ISO 22301, understanding the role of management review, and effectively managing non-conformities. By establishing robust auditing and review processes, you can continuously assess the performance of your BCMS and identify areas for improvement.

Chapter 9: The Continual Improvement Process The journey towards business

continuity excellence does not end with implementation. It requires a commitment to continuous improvement. In this chapter, we explore how ISO 22301 can be utilized as a tool to foster continual improvement in your organization's business continuity management. We discuss the importance of monitoring, measuring, analyzing, and evaluating the performance of your BCMS, and how to use these insights to drive ongoing enhancements and optimize your resilience.

Chapter 10: Case Studies of Successful ISO 22301 Implementation To inspire and

guide you further, Chapter 10 presents real-world case studies of organizations that have successfully implemented ISO 22301. These case studies offer valuable insights and lessons learned, showcasing how different organizations overcame challenges, leveraged resources, and reaped the benefits of ISO 22301. By examining these examples, you can gain practical knowledge and inspiration to navigate your own implementation journey.

Throughout Part II, each chapter is accompanied by practical exercises and self-assessment tools. These tools are designed to help you apply the concepts and principles discussed within your own organization, ensuring a hands-on and impactful learning experience.

As we progress through the chapters, we will equip you with the knowledge and strategies necessary to overcome challenges, integrate ISO 22301 with other management systems, navigate the certification process, and maintain long-term compliance.

We invite you to dive into Part II, embrace the practical aspects of ISO 22301 implementation, and pave the way for a resilient and prepared future for your organization. Let's embark on this journey together as we unlock the potential of ISO 22301 for effective business continuity management.

CHAPTER 6
Resources for ISO 22301 Implementation

6.1 Introduction

The crucial role of resources in the successful implementation of ISO 22301

esources play a crucial role in the successful implementation of ISO 22301 and resilient BCMS. Here are some key aspects highlighting the importance of resources:

1. **Personnel**: Skilled and knowledgeable personnel are essential for the successful implementation of ISO 22301. Assigning dedicated resources with expertise in business continuity management can drive the implementation process, conduct risk assessments, develop policies and procedures, and coordinate training and awareness programs. These individuals should be capable of leading the BCMS implementation efforts and collaborating with other stakeholders across the organization.

2. **Time and Commitment**: Implementing ISO 22301 requires time and commitment from personnel at all levels. Organizations need to allocate sufficient time for planning, conducting risk assessments, developing policies and procedures, training employees, and conducting regular audits. Top management's commitment is critical in allocating the necessary time and resources, as well as demonstrating their support throughout the implementation process.

3. **Financial Investment**: Implementing ISO 22301 may involve financial investments, such as training programs, technology solutions, consultancy services, and the allocation of dedicated budget for business continuity activities. Adequate financial resources are necessary to establish and maintain the BCMS effectively. Organizations should consider the long-term benefits and return on investment associated with ISO 22301 compliance in making financial decisions.

4. **Technology and Infrastructure**: The effective implementation of ISO 22301 often relies on leveraging technology solutions to support various BCMS activities. This may include risk assessment tools, business continuity planning software, incident management systems, communication platforms, and data backup solutions. Adequate technology infrastructure, including hardware, software, and network capabilities, is necessary to support the implementation and operation of the BCMS.

5. **Training and Education**: Building knowledge and competence among employees is vital for the successful implementation of ISO 22301. Resources should be allocated for training programs and awareness initiatives to ensure that employees understand their roles and responsibilities, are familiar with the BCMS processes and procedures, and possess the necessary skills to respond effectively during incidents or disruptions. Training should be ongoing to keep employees up to date with the evolving BCMS requirements.

6. **Expertise and External Support**: Organizations may require external expertise or consultancy services to ensure a smooth and effective implementation of ISO 22301. Engaging external professionals or consultants who specialize in business continuity management can provide guidance, expertise, and practical insights to navigate challenges, develop appropriate strategies, and ensure compliance with the standard.

7. **Documentation and Information Management**: The documentation requirements of ISO 22301 necessitate resources for creating, organizing, updating, and maintaining documentation. This includes developing policies, procedures, plans, and records, as well as establishing effective document control processes and information management systems. Dedicated resources should be assigned to manage and ensure the accuracy, accessibility, and currency of the BCMS documentation.

By allocating the necessary resources, organizations demonstrate their commitment to business continuity and ensure the effective implementation of ISO 22301. Adequate resources enhance the organization's ability to identify and mitigate risks, respond to incidents, and recover critical functions in a timely manner. They enable the organization to build a resilient BCMS that protects the organization, its employees, customers, and stakeholders during disruptions.

An overview of the types of resources needed

Implementing ISO 22301 and establishing a robust Business Continuity Management System (BCMS) requires various types of resources. These resources encompass personnel, technology, financial investments, and documentation. Here's an overview of the types of resources needed:

1. **Personnel Resources**:

- Business Continuity Manager or Coordinator: A dedicated individual responsible for overseeing the implementation, maintenance, and improvement of the BCMS.

- Business Continuity Team: A cross-functional team comprising representatives from various departments or functions who contribute to the BCMS implementation and operation.

- Subject Matter Experts: Personnel with expertise in risk assessment, business impact analysis, incident response, crisis management, and other aspects of business continuity.

☐ **Trained Employees:** Employees who receive training on their roles and responsibilities within the BCMS, including incident response, recovery procedures, and business continuity best practices.

2. **Financial Resources:**

☐ **Budget:** Allocating financial resources to cover the costs associated with implementing and maintaining the BCMS, including training, technology, consultancy services, and testing exercises.

☐ **Technology Investment:** Funding for acquiring and maintaining technology solutions that support the BCMS, such as business continuity planning software, notification systems, incident management tools, and data backup solutions.

☐ **External Expertise:** Budgeting for engaging external consultants or experts who can provide guidance and support during the implementation process.

3. **Technology Resources:**

☐ **Hardware:** Computers, servers, network infrastructure, and other hardware necessary to support the BCMS implementation and operation.

☐ **Software Applications:** Business continuity planning software, risk assessment tools, incident management systems, communication platforms, and other software solutions that facilitate BCMS activities.

☐ **Communication Tools:** Mass notification systems, emergency communication platforms, and collaboration tools to enable effective communication during incidents or disruptions.

☐ **Data Backup Solutions:** Technology solutions for regular data backups, secure storage, and recovery mechanisms to protect critical information and systems.

4. **Documentation Resources:**

☐ **BCMS Policies and Procedures:** Development of policies, procedures, and guidelines that outline the organization's approach to business continuity and ensure compliance with ISO 22301.

☐ **Business Continuity Plans (BCPs):** Documentation of specific plans and procedures to guide response and recovery activities during incidents or disruptions.

☐ **Records and Documentation Management:** Establishing processes and systems to create, organize, update, and maintain documentation, ensuring accessibility, accuracy, and version control.

It's important to allocate the necessary resources to support the successful implementation and operation of the BCMS. These resources enable organizations to effectively identify and manage risks, establish appropriate response and recovery procedures, and maintain a resilient business continuity posture. By leveraging the right mix of personnel, technology, financial investments, and documentation resources, organizations can build a robust BCMS that safeguards critical operations and enhances their ability to withstand disruptions.

6.2 Human Resources

The skills and competencies required for ISO 22301 implementation

Implementing ISO 22301 requires a range of skills and competencies to ensure the successful establishment and operation of a Business Continuity Management System (BCMS). Here are some key skills and competencies that are beneficial for ISO 22301 implementation:

1. **Business Continuity Management (BCM) Knowledge**: A solid understanding of the principles, concepts, and practices of BCM is crucial. This includes knowledge of risk assessment, business impact analysis, incident response, crisis management, and recovery strategies. Familiarity with ISO 22301 and its requirements is essential for effective implementation.

2. **Risk Management**: Proficiency in risk management is important for identifying, assessing, and prioritizing risks to the organization's business continuity. This involves the ability to analyze and evaluate potential threats, vulnerabilities, and impacts, as well as develop risk treatment plans and mitigation strategies.

3. **Project Management**: Strong project management skills are necessary to plan, execute, and monitor the implementation of ISO 22301 effectively. This includes developing project plans, defining deliverables and timelines, coordinating resources, managing stakeholders, and ensuring successful project completion.

4. **Communication and Stakeholder Engagement**: Excellent communication skills are vital for engaging and collaborating with stakeholders at all levels of the organization. This includes effectively communicating the purpose, benefits, and requirements of ISO 22301, facilitating training and awareness programs, and fostering a culture of resilience.

5. **Analytical and Problem-Solving Skills**: The ability to analyze complex situations, identify gaps or areas for improvement, and develop practical solutions is critical. This includes conducting gap analyses, identifying root causes of issues or non-conformities, and implementing corrective and preventive actions.

6. **Change Management**: Implementing ISO 22301 often involves changes to processes, procedures, and organizational culture. Proficiency in change management helps navigate resistance to change, communicate the need for

change, and ensure successful adoption of new practices within the organization.

7. **Audit and Compliance Knowledge**: Understanding auditing principles and compliance requirements is valuable for conducting internal audits, monitoring the effectiveness of the BCMS, and ensuring compliance with ISO 22301.

8. **Training and Facilitation Skills**: The ability to design and deliver training programs and facilitate workshops is essential for educating employees and stakeholders about their roles and responsibilities within the BCMS. Effective training and facilitation skills ensure a smooth implementation process and promote engagement and understanding.

9. **Continuous Improvement Mindset**: Embracing a mindset of continuous improvement is vital for sustaining and enhancing the BCMS over time. This involves actively seeking opportunities for improvement, collecting and analyzing performance data, and driving ongoing refinement and optimization of the BCMS.

While individuals with these skills and competencies are valuable for ISO 22301 implementation, it is important to note that teamwork and collaboration across various departments and functions are equally important. In many cases, organizations may choose to invest in training and professional development programs to build these skills internally or seek external expertise through consultants or BCM specialists to support the implementation process.

Developing a dedicated BCMS team

Developing a dedicated Business Continuity Management System (BCMS) team is crucial for the successful implementation and ongoing management of ISO 22301. This team will play a central role in driving the BCMS efforts, coordinating activities, and ensuring the organization's resilience. Here are some key considerations for developing a dedicated BCMS team:

1. **Identify Roles and Responsibilities**: Determine the specific roles and responsibilities needed within the BCMS team. This may include a Business Continuity Manager or Coordinator, subject matter experts, representatives from different departments or functions, and individuals responsible for specific BCMS activities such as risk assessment, business impact analysis, plan development, training, and testing.

2. **Define Team Structure**: Determine the team's structure based on the organization's size, complexity, and BCMS requirements. Consider factors such as reporting lines, coordination mechanisms, and the need for cross-functional collaboration. Clearly define team members' reporting relationships, authority, and accountability to ensure smooth operations and effective decision-making.

3. **Establish Leadership**: Designate a leader for the BCMS team who will have overall responsibility for driving the implementation and maintenance of the

BCMS. The leader should have the necessary knowledge, skills, and authority to guide the team and influence stakeholders across the organization.

4. **Ensure Adequate Resources**: Allocate sufficient resources to the BCMS team to support their activities effectively. This includes providing dedicated time, personnel, training, and budgetary provisions. Adequate resources enable the team to focus on their responsibilities, conduct necessary training and awareness programs, and implement the BCMS activities with success.

5. **Cross-Functional Representation**: Include representatives from different departments or functions within the BCMS team. This ensures that the BCMS is aligned with the organization's overall operations, captures diverse perspectives, and fosters collaboration and information sharing. Consider involving individuals from IT, human resources, facilities management, legal, and other relevant areas.

6. **Training and Development**: Invest in training and development opportunities for the BCMS team members to enhance their skills and knowledge in business continuity management. This may include specialized training on ISO 22301, risk assessment methodologies, incident response, crisis management, and other relevant areas. Ongoing professional development keeps the team members up to date with industry best practices and enhances their effectiveness.

7. **Clear Communication and Reporting**: Establish clear communication channels and reporting mechanisms within the BCMS team. Regular team meetings, progress updates, and documentation of actions and decisions facilitate transparency, accountability, and efficient coordination. Effective communication ensures that team members are aligned, informed, and engaged in the BCMS implementation.

8. **Collaboration with Stakeholders**: Foster collaboration with stakeholders across the organization. Engage senior management, department heads, and employees at all levels to promote their involvement and support for the BCMS. Seek their input, gather feedback, and ensure alignment with organizational goals and objectives.

9. **Continual Improvement Mindset**: Instill a culture of continual improvement within the BCMS team. Encourage team members to proactively identify opportunities for enhancement, learn from incidents and exercises, and drive ongoing refinement of the BCMS. Foster a learning environment that promotes sharing of best practices, lessons learned, and innovative approaches.

By developing a dedicated BCMS team, organizations can ensure focused attention on business continuity management, effective coordination of BCMS activities, and sustained commitment to ISO 22301 compliance. The team serves as a driving force behind the successful implementation and continuous improvement of the BCMS, ultimately enhancing the organization's resilience and ability to respond to disruptions.

The importance of training and development

Training and development play a crucial role in the successful implementation and maintenance of ISO 22301 and the overall effectiveness of a Business Continuity Management System (BCMS). Here are some key reasons highlighting the importance of training and development:

1. **Knowledge and Skills Enhancement**: Training provides employees with the necessary knowledge and skills to understand and fulfill their roles and responsibilities within the BCMS. It helps them gain a deeper understanding of business continuity concepts, ISO 22301 requirements, risk assessment methodologies, incident response protocols, and other relevant topics. By enhancing their knowledge and skills, employees are better equipped to contribute effectively to the BCMS implementation and operation.

2. **Improved BCMS Performance**: Well-trained employees are more capable of implementing the BCMS effectively, following established procedures, and contributing to the success of the system. Training helps employees understand the purpose and benefits of the BCMS, enabling them to align their activities with the organization's goals and objectives. This leads to improved performance in risk management, incident response, business continuity planning, and other BCMS-related activities.

3. **Standard Compliance**: ISO 22301 requires organizations to provide appropriate training and awareness programs to ensure employees are aware of their roles and responsibilities within the BCMS. By investing in training, organizations demonstrate their commitment to meeting these requirements and achieving compliance with the standard. Properly trained employees contribute to the effective implementation of ISO 22301, making the organization better prepared for disruptions and improving its ability to recover.

4. **Culture of Resilience**: Training and development programs create a culture of resilience within the organization. By educating employees about the importance of business continuity, the potential risks they may face, and the measures in place to mitigate those risks, organizations foster a proactive and prepared mindset among their workforce. This culture of resilience promotes a sense of ownership and responsibility for business continuity throughout the organization.

5. **Employee Engagement and Motivation**: Providing training and development opportunities demonstrates an organization's commitment to employee growth and professional development. It enhances employee engagement, job satisfaction, and morale, as employees feel valued and supported in their roles. Engaged and motivated employees are more likely to actively participate in BCMS activities, contribute innovative ideas, and take ownership of their responsibilities within the system.

6. **Adaptation to Changing Circumstances**: Training and development programs help employees stay current with evolving best practices, industry trends, and emerging risks. This enables them to adapt to changing circumstances and respond effectively to new challenges. Ongoing training ensures that employees are equipped with the necessary knowledge and skills

to address emerging threats, implement updated procedures, and continually improve the BCMS.

7. **Knowledge Transfer and Succession Planning**: Training programs facilitate knowledge transfer within the organization. By sharing expertise and experience through training sessions, organizations ensure that the BCMS knowledge and skills are not concentrated in a few individuals but are spread across the organization. This helps in succession planning, as employees can be groomed to take on key roles within the BCMS, ensuring its continuity and long-term success.

8. **External Recognition and Stakeholder Confidence**: Well-trained employees contribute to the overall professionalism and competence of the BCMS. This enhances external recognition and stakeholder confidence in the organization's ability to manage business continuity effectively. Certification bodies, regulators, customers, and other stakeholders value organizations that invest in training and development, as it demonstrates a commitment to excellence and continuous improvement.

Investing in training and development programs for employees involved in the BCMS is essential for building a capable and resilient workforce. It enables organizations to implement ISO 22301 effectively, adapt to changing circumstances, and maintain a high level of performance in business continuity management.

6.3 Technological Tools

Identification of technological resources needed for implementing and maintaining BCMS

Implementing and maintaining a Business Continuity Management System (BCMS) requires leveraging various technological resources. Here are some key technological tools and resources needed for implementing and maintaining a BCMS:

1. **Business Continuity Planning (BCP) Software**: BCP software helps organizations develop, manage, and update their business continuity plans. It provides a centralized platform for creating plan templates, documenting recovery procedures, conducting plan reviews, and tracking plan changes. BCP software streamlines the planning process and ensures that plans are easily accessible, up-to-date, and readily available during incidents.

2. **Risk Assessment Tools**: Risk assessment tools assist in identifying, analyzing, and evaluating risks to the organization's business continuity. These tools facilitate the assessment of potential threats, vulnerabilities, and impacts, and help in prioritizing risk treatment strategies. Risk assessment software often includes features for risk scoring, risk register management, and reporting.

3. **Notification and Communication Systems**: Notification and communication systems enable organizations to quickly disseminate critical information to employees, stakeholders, and relevant parties during incidents or disruptions. These systems can include mass notification platforms,

emergency communication tools, and real-time communication channels such as mobile apps, SMS, email, and voice alerts.

4. **Incident Management Tools**: Incident management tools help organizations effectively manage and respond to incidents or disruptions. These tools provide a centralized platform to document incident details, assign tasks, track progress, and communicate updates. Incident management software enhances coordination, facilitates collaboration among response teams, and enables timely decision-making.

5. **Document Management Systems**: Document management systems assist in organizing, storing, and retrieving BCMS-related documents and information. These systems provide version control, access controls, and document sharing capabilities, ensuring that the latest versions of policies, procedures, plans, and records are readily available to authorized personnel.

6. **Training and Learning Management Systems**: Training and learning management systems facilitate the delivery and tracking of BCMS training programs and employee awareness initiatives. These systems enable the creation of e-learning modules, assessments, and tracking of employee progress. Training and learning management systems help ensure consistent and comprehensive training for employees involved in the BCMS.

7. **Data Backup and Recovery Solutions**: Data backup and recovery solutions are essential for safeguarding critical data and ensuring its availability during and after incidents or disruptions. These solutions include regular backups of critical systems and data, secure off-site storage, and mechanisms for data restoration and recovery.

8. **Monitoring and Alerting Systems**: Monitoring and alerting systems provide real-time monitoring of critical infrastructure, systems, and processes. These systems can include network monitoring tools, environmental sensors, security monitoring systems, and other monitoring solutions. They help detect and notify stakeholders of potential issues, anomalies, or breaches that may impact business continuity.

9. **Collaboration and Workflow Tools**: Collaboration and workflow tools facilitate communication, collaboration, and task management among BCMS team members and stakeholders. These tools help streamline processes, track action items, and enable efficient collaboration during plan development, exercises, incident response, and recovery efforts.

It's important to assess the organization's specific needs, consider budgetary constraints, and select technological resources that align with the BCMS objectives and processes. Integrating these technological tools into the BCMS enhances efficiency, accuracy, communication, and coordination, ultimately strengthening the organization's ability to manage and respond to disruptions effectively.

- Guidance on selecting the right BCMS software and tools

Selecting the right Business Continuity Management System (BCMS) software and tools is crucial for effectively implementing and maintaining your BCMS. Here are some key considerations and guidance to help you in the selection process:

1. **Define Your Requirements**: Begin by clearly defining your organization's specific BCMS requirements. This includes identifying the functionalities, features, and capabilities you need from the software and tools. Consider your organization's size, complexity, industry, and specific BCMS objectives to determine the must-have features.

2. **Conduct a Needs Assessment**: Perform a thorough needs assessment to understand the specific challenges and gaps in your current BCMS. Identify the pain points, areas for improvement, and the desired outcomes you want to achieve with the software and tools. This assessment will help you align your requirements with the right solutions.

3. **Research and Evaluate**: Research the market for BCMS software and tools. Look for reputable vendors and solutions that align with your requirements. Evaluate their features, functionalities, user interface, scalability, and compatibility with your existing systems. Consider factors such as ease of use, customization options, reporting capabilities, and integration possibilities.

4. **Vendor Reputation and Support**: Consider the reputation and track record of the vendors you are evaluating. Look for customer reviews, case studies, and testimonials to gauge the vendor's credibility. Additionally, assess their customer support and service offerings, as you will likely need ongoing support during the implementation and maintenance phases.

5. **Consider User-Friendliness**: Ensure that the software and tools are user-friendly and intuitive for your BCMS team and other end-users. Ease of use is essential to encourage adoption and maximize the benefits of the software. Look for solutions that have a clean and intuitive interface, as well as comprehensive user guides and training resources.

6. **Compatibility and Integration**: Assess the compatibility of the software and tools with your existing technology infrastructure, such as operating systems, databases, and communication systems. Ensure that the solutions can integrate with other relevant systems, such as incident management systems, notification systems, or document management platforms, to streamline your BCMS operations.

7. **Scalability**: Consider the scalability of the software and tools to accommodate the growth and evolving needs of your organization. Evaluate whether the solutions can handle an increasing number of users, expanding data volumes, and additional functionalities as your BCMS matures over time.

8. **Cost and Value for Money**: Consider the total cost of ownership, including licensing fees, implementation costs, ongoing maintenance, and support charges. Assess the value for money by evaluating the features, capabilities, and benefits of the software and tools against their cost. Consider the return on investment and long-term benefits that the solutions can provide to your BCMS.

9. **Trial and Demo**: Whenever possible, request trials or demos of the shortlisted software and tools. This will allow you to explore the functionalities, user experience, and suitability of the solutions firsthand. Engage key stakeholders and end-users in the trial process to gather their feedback and ensure their needs are met.

10. **References and Recommendations**: Reach out to other organizations or professionals in your industry who have implemented similar BCMS software and tools. Seek their insights, experiences, and recommendations to inform your decision-making process.

Remember that selecting BCMS software and tools is a significant decision that will impact the effectiveness and efficiency of your BCMS implementation. Take your time to evaluate and compare options, involve key stakeholders, and choose the solutions that best align with your organization's needs and goals.

6.4 Financial Resources

Estimation of the financial investment required for ISO 22301 implementation

Estimating the financial investment required for ISO 22301 implementation can vary depending on several factors, including the size and complexity of your organization, the current state of your business continuity practices, and the level of compliance you aim to achieve. Here are some key areas to consider when estimating the financial investment for ISO 22301 implementation:

1. **Gap Analysis and Assessment**: Conducting a comprehensive gap analysis to identify the existing gaps between your current practices and the requirements of ISO 22301 is an important first step. This assessment helps determine the level of effort and resources needed to bring your organization into compliance. The cost of conducting the gap analysis may include internal or external consultants, tools, and resources required for data collection and analysis.

2. **Training and Education**: Investing in training and education is crucial to ensure that employees and key stakeholders understand the principles and requirements of ISO 22301. This may involve the cost of conducting training sessions, hiring external trainers, developing training materials, and providing ongoing awareness programs. Consider both initial training costs and ongoing training needs as the BCMS evolves.

3. **Documentation and Policy Development**: Developing the necessary policies, procedures, and documentation to support your BCMS implementation incurs costs. This includes the time and effort required to draft, review, and finalize policies and procedures, as well as the cost of tools or software for document management and version control.

4. **Technology and Tools**: Implementing technological resources, such as business continuity planning software, risk assessment tools, incident management systems, or notification systems, may require a financial

investment. Consider the costs of software licenses, implementation, customization, training, and ongoing maintenance and support.

5. **Resource Allocation**: Allocating dedicated personnel and their time to the BCMS implementation is an important consideration. This may involve additional staffing or the reallocation of existing resources within the organization. Evaluate the financial impact of personnel costs, including salaries, benefits, and any additional training or certifications required.

6. **Consultancy and External Support**: Depending on your organization's size, complexity, and internal capabilities, you may require external consultants or experts to support the ISO 22301 implementation. Consider the cost of engaging external consultants for guidance, assessment, training, or project management support.

7. **Internal Audits and Certification**: Conducting internal audits and seeking ISO 22301 certification requires financial investment. This includes the cost of internal audit resources, certification body fees, external audits (if required), and ongoing surveillance and recertification costs.

8. **Exercises and Testing**: Regularly testing the BCMS through exercises and simulations is essential for verifying its effectiveness. Consider the cost of planning and conducting tabletop exercises, functional exercises, or full-scale simulations. This may include costs associated with scenario development, facilitation, evaluation, and subsequent improvements.

It's important to note that the financial investment for ISO 22301 implementation can vary significantly depending on the organization's size, industry, and existing business continuity practices. Conduct a thorough assessment of your organization's specific needs and requirements to estimate the financial investment accurately. Develop a budget that considers both the initial implementation costs and ongoing maintenance, training, and improvement expenses to ensure a sustainable BCMS.

Understanding the cost implications and the return on investment

Understanding the cost implications and return on investment (ROI) of ISO 22301 implementation is essential for making informed decisions and securing necessary resources. Here are some key considerations:

1. **Cost Implications**:

    ☐ Implementation Costs: Consider the costs associated with conducting a gap analysis, developing policies and procedures, training, and acquiring necessary tools or technologies.

    ☐ Training and Awareness: Allocate budget for training programs, workshops, and awareness initiatives to educate employees and stakeholders about ISO 22301 requirements.

    ☐ Technology Investments: Evaluate the cost of implementing and maintaining technological resources such as BCMS software, risk assessment tools, or communication systems.

☐ **Internal Audits and Certification**: Budget for internal audit resources, certification fees, and ongoing surveillance and recertification costs.

☐ **Resource Allocation**: Consider the financial implications of dedicating personnel to BCMS activities, including additional staffing or reallocating existing resources.

2. **Return on Investment (ROI)**:

☐ **Enhanced Resilience**: ISO 22301 helps organizations strengthen their resilience to potential disruptions, reducing the financial impact of incidents and enabling faster recovery. This can result in cost savings by minimizing revenue loss, reducing downtime, and preserving customer trust.

☐ **Regulatory Compliance**: ISO 22301 certification can help organizations meet regulatory requirements and enhance their reputation, potentially leading to increased business opportunities and market competitiveness.

☐ **Improved Efficiency**: Implementing ISO 22301 promotes streamlined processes, effective risk management, and standardized procedures, leading to operational efficiency, cost reductions, and improved resource utilization.

☐ **Customer Confidence**: Demonstrating compliance with ISO 22301 can enhance customer confidence and trust, attracting new customers and retaining existing ones.

☐ **Insurance Premiums**: Some insurance companies offer reduced premiums or favorable terms to organizations with ISO 22301 certification, resulting in potential cost savings.

To evaluate the ROI, consider both tangible and intangible benefits. Tangible benefits include measurable cost savings, revenue increases, or reduced insurance premiums. Intangible benefits, such as improved brand reputation, enhanced customer loyalty, and stakeholder trust, may be more challenging to quantify but still contribute to the overall ROI.

Conduct a cost-benefit analysis, comparing the anticipated costs with the expected benefits over time. This analysis can help justify the financial investment, secure necessary resources, and provide a basis for decision-making. It's important to periodically evaluate and reassess the ROI as the BCMS evolves and matures, considering ongoing maintenance costs, improvements, and business changes.

Remember, the ROI of ISO 22301 implementation extends beyond financial aspects and encompasses improved organizational resilience, risk mitigation, and stakeholder confidence, which are invaluable for long-term business success.

6.5 External Resources

The role of consultants and external experts in ISO 22301 implementation

Consultants and external experts play a significant role in supporting organizations during ISO 22301 implementation. Their expertise and experience can provide valuable guidance, enhance the effectiveness of the BCMS, and accelerate the implementation process. Here are some key roles and benefits of consultants and external experts in ISO 22301 implementation:

1. **Subject Matter Expertise**: Consultants and external experts possess in-depth knowledge of ISO 22301 requirements, best practices, and industry trends. They can provide expert advice and guidance on interpreting the standard, aligning it with organizational objectives, and tailoring the implementation approach to specific business needs. Their expertise ensures a robust and compliant BCMS.

2. **Gap Analysis and Readiness Assessments**: Consultants can conduct thorough gap analyses and readiness assessments to evaluate an organization's current state of business continuity practices against ISO 22301 requirements. They identify gaps, strengths, and areas for improvement, providing a clear roadmap for implementation and helping prioritize actions.

3. **Policy and Procedure Development**: Consultants can assist in developing BCMS policies, procedures, and documentation that align with ISO 22301. They bring knowledge of industry best practices and can help tailor policies and procedures to the organization's specific context. Their input ensures that the documentation meets the standard's requirements and reflects industry norms.

4. **Training and Education**: Consultants can provide specialized training and education on ISO 22301, business continuity management, risk assessment, incident response, and other relevant areas. They deliver informative sessions, workshops, and customized training materials to educate employees and key stakeholders about the standard's principles, requirements, and implementation strategies.

5. **Project Management Support**: Implementing ISO 22301 involves coordination, planning, and resource management. Consultants can provide project management support, ensuring that the implementation process remains on track, milestones are achieved, and deliverables are met within the designated timeframes. They help organizations streamline the implementation process and keep stakeholders informed.

6. **External Audits and Certification**: Consultants can assist organizations in preparing for external audits and achieving ISO 22301 certification. They can conduct internal audits, identify areas of non-compliance, and provide recommendations for improvement. Their experience and understanding of certification requirements ensure that organizations are well-prepared and increase their chances of successful certification.

7. **Industry Insights and Benchmarking**: Consultants stay updated with the latest industry practices, benchmarks, and emerging trends in business continuity management. They bring valuable insights into how other organizations have successfully implemented ISO 22301 and can provide benchmarking opportunities to gauge an organization's progress and maturity in BCMS implementation.

8. **Troubleshooting and Problem-solving**: Consultants can help organizations overcome challenges and roadblocks during the implementation process. Their experience in dealing with various scenarios and their problem-solving abilities enable them to provide practical solutions to address specific issues that may arise during ISO 22301 implementation.

9. **Cost and Time Efficiency**: Engaging consultants can save organizations time and effort by leveraging their expertise and specialized knowledge. They bring efficiency to the implementation process, ensuring that resources are utilized effectively, and the BCMS is implemented in a timely manner. This allows organizations to focus on their core business while benefiting from the consultants' dedicated support.

When engaging consultants and external experts, it is important to select reputable professionals or consulting firms with a proven track record in business continuity management and ISO 22301 implementation. Ensure they have relevant certifications and experience working with organizations similar to yours. Clearly define the scope of work, deliverables, and expectations in the consulting engagement to ensure a mutually beneficial relationship.

Guidelines for selecting and working with consultants

When selecting and working with consultants for ISO 22301 implementation, it's important to follow some guidelines to ensure a successful partnership. Here are some key guidelines to consider:

1. **Define Your Needs**: Clearly define your organization's needs, objectives, and expectations for engaging a consultant. Identify specific areas where you require assistance, such as gap analysis, policy development, training, or certification support. Having a clear understanding of your needs will help you find a consultant with the right expertise and experience.

2. **Evaluate Consultant Expertise**: Assess the consultant's expertise and experience in ISO 22301 implementation and business continuity management. Look for relevant certifications, industry experience, and successful track records in assisting organizations similar to yours. Consider requesting case studies, references, or client testimonials to verify their capabilities.

3. **Establish Clear Scope of Work**: Define the scope of work and deliverables in a detailed agreement or contract. Clearly outline the tasks, timelines, milestones, and expected outcomes. This ensures that both parties have a shared understanding of the project and helps avoid misunderstandings or scope creep.

4. **Effective Communication and Collaboration**: Establish open and effective communication channels with the consultant. Regularly communicate your organization's needs, provide necessary information, and actively participate in discussions and decision-making. Encourage the consultant to ask questions and seek clarifications to ensure alignment and understanding.

5. **Collaborative Approach**: Foster a collaborative working relationship with the consultant. Engage key stakeholders from your organization in the process and involve them in discussions and decision-making. Collaboratively work with the consultant to develop policies, procedures, and other deliverables, ensuring that they are tailored to your organization's unique needs.

6. **Transparency and Trust**: Maintain transparency and build trust with the consultant. Share relevant information, such as existing business continuity practices, challenges, and constraints. Establish a relationship based on trust, allowing the consultant to provide objective advice, raise concerns, and propose effective solutions.

7. **Regular Progress Reviews**: Schedule regular progress reviews to track the consultant's work and ensure that project milestones are being met. Review and provide feedback on deliverables in a timely manner. Regular reviews enable you to address any issues or concerns promptly and ensure alignment with your organization's objectives.

8. **Knowledge Transfer and Training**: Seek knowledge transfer from the consultant to your internal team. Encourage the consultant to share expertise, provide training sessions, and transfer relevant skills and knowledge to your employees. This helps build internal capabilities and ensures that the benefits of the consultant's work are sustained in the long term.

9. **Continuous Improvement**: Foster a culture of continuous improvement throughout the engagement. Encourage the consultant to provide recommendations for ongoing enhancement of your BCMS beyond the immediate project. Leverage their expertise to identify areas for improvement, implement best practices, and drive continuous improvement in your organization's business continuity practices.

10. **Evaluate Results**: Regularly evaluate the consultant's performance and the outcomes of their work. Assess whether the agreed-upon deliverables are being met and whether the consultant's services have provided value to your organization. Provide constructive feedback to the consultant, as this can help improve future engagements or assist other organizations in their selection process.

By following these guidelines, you can maximize the effectiveness of the consultant engagement and ensure a successful collaboration that supports your ISO 22301 implementation efforts.

Leveraging external training programs and workshops

Leveraging external training programs and workshops can be beneficial for organizations seeking to enhance their knowledge and skills in ISO 22301 implementation. Here are some guidelines for effectively utilizing external training programs and workshops:

1. **Identify Training Needs**: Assess your organization's specific training needs related to ISO 22301 implementation. Determine the areas where additional knowledge or skills are required, such as understanding the standard's requirements, risk assessment methodologies, incident response planning, or conducting business impact analysis. This helps you target the right training programs and workshops.

2. **Research Training Providers**: Conduct thorough research to identify reputable training providers that offer ISO 22301-related courses, workshops, or certification programs. Consider factors such as the provider's reputation, experience, training content, trainers' expertise, and the applicability of the training to your organization's context.

3. **Course Selection**: Select training programs or workshops that align with your organization's specific needs. Look for courses that cover the relevant aspects of ISO 22301, including policy development, risk assessment, business impact analysis, plan development, and testing. Consider whether the training is suitable for different roles and levels within your organization, from top management to operational staff.

4. **Customized Training**: In some cases, organizations may require customized training programs tailored to their specific needs and challenges. Engage with training providers who can customize their offerings to address your organization's unique requirements. Customized training ensures that the content and examples provided are directly applicable to your industry and business context.

5. **Trainer Expertise**: Assess the expertise and experience of the trainers delivering the programs or workshops. Look for trainers who have practical experience in ISO 22301 implementation, business continuity management, and related fields. Trainers with real-world experience can provide valuable insights and practical knowledge during the training sessions.

6. **Training Delivery Modes**: Consider the different delivery modes available, such as in-person workshops, virtual training, or self-paced e-learning modules. Evaluate which mode suits your organization's needs, taking into account factors such as the availability of participants, geographical locations, and preferred learning styles.

7. **Participant Engagement**: Encourage active participation and engagement from participants during the training sessions. This can be achieved through interactive exercises, group discussions, case studies, and hands-on activities. Active engagement helps reinforce learning, encourages knowledge sharing, and facilitates the practical application of concepts to real-world scenarios.

8. **Post-Training Support**: Inquire about post-training support provided by the training provider. This could include access to resources, additional materials, or follow-up consultations to address any questions or challenges

that arise after the training. Post-training support enhances the value of the training and helps reinforce the concepts learned.

9. **Evaluation and Feedback**: Evaluate the effectiveness of the training programs or workshops through participant feedback and post-training assessments. Encourage participants to provide constructive feedback on the training content, delivery, and overall experience. This feedback can help you assess the effectiveness of the training and identify areas for improvement.

10. **Continuous Learning**: Emphasize the importance of continuous learning within your organization. Encourage participants to apply the knowledge gained from the training in their day-to-day roles and share their learnings with their teams. Foster a culture of ongoing professional development and encourage employees to seek additional training opportunities to deepen their understanding of ISO 22301 and enhance their BCMS skills.

By leveraging external training programs and workshops effectively, organizations can enhance their understanding of ISO 22301, develop key skills, and foster a culture of business continuity within their teams. This contributes to the successful implementation and maintenance of an effective BCMS.

6.6 Time

An overview of the time frame for ISO 22301 implementation

The time frame for ISO 22301 implementation can vary depending on various factors, including the size and complexity of the organization, the current state of business continuity practices, available resources, and the level of commitment from key stakeholders. While the actual time required will differ for each organization, here is a general overview of the time frame for ISO 22301 implementation:

1. **Initial Assessment and Planning**: This phase involves conducting an initial assessment of the organization's current business continuity practices and readiness for ISO 22301 implementation. It includes identifying gaps, establishing project objectives, and creating an implementation plan. Depending on the organization's size and complexity, this phase typically takes several weeks to a few months.

2. **Policy and Procedure Development**: Developing the necessary policies, procedures, and documentation to support the BCMS implementation can take several weeks to a few months. This includes drafting, reviewing, and finalizing policies, procedures, and other documentation to ensure compliance with ISO 22301 requirements.

3. **Risk Assessment and Business Impact Analysis**: Conducting a comprehensive risk assessment and business impact analysis (BIA) is crucial for identifying potential threats, vulnerabilities, and impacts to the organization. This phase can range from a few weeks to several months, depending on the organization's size, complexity, and available resources.

4. **BCMS Implementation**: Implementing the BCMS involves establishing and operationalizing the key components, such as developing business continuity

plans, defining roles and responsibilities, conducting training and awareness programs, and implementing necessary technological tools. The time required for implementation can vary depending on the organization's size and complexity but generally ranges from several months to a year.

5. **Testing and Exercising**: Regularly testing and exercising the BCMS is essential to evaluate its effectiveness and ensure readiness for potential incidents. This phase involves planning, conducting, and evaluating tabletop exercises, functional exercises, or full-scale simulations. The frequency and scope of testing and exercising will depend on the organization's risk profile and industry requirements.

6. **Internal Audits and Certification Readiness**: Conducting internal audits to assess the BCMS's compliance with ISO 22301 requirements is an important step before pursuing certification. The time required for internal audits will depend on the organization's size and complexity. Preparing for certification readiness may involve additional time for addressing any non-compliances identified during the internal audits.

7. **External Certification Process**: Pursuing ISO 22301 certification involves engaging a certification body, which will assess the organization's compliance with the standard's requirements. The certification process typically includes a formal application, documentation review, on-site audits, and a certification decision. The duration for the external certification process can vary depending on the certification body and their specific processes.

It's important to note that the time frame for ISO 22301 implementation can be influenced by internal factors such as the availability of resources, organizational culture, and the level of management support. It is recommended to establish a realistic implementation timeline based on your organization's specific circumstances and allocate sufficient resources to ensure a thorough and effective implementation of the BCMS.

Additionally, ISO 22301 is a journey of continuous improvement, and organizations should plan for ongoing monitoring, maintenance, and enhancement of their BCMS even after achieving certification. This ensures that the BCMS remains effective and relevant as the organization evolves and new risks emerge.

Understanding the factors influencing the timeline

The timeline for ISO 22301 implementation can be influenced by various factors. It's important to consider these factors when estimating the time required for implementing the standard. Here are some key factors that can influence the timeline:

1. **Organization Size and Complexity**: The size and complexity of the organization play a significant role in determining the implementation timeline. Larger organizations or those with multiple business units may require more time to coordinate and align various stakeholders, processes, and systems.

2. **Current State of Business Continuity Practices**: Organizations with well-established business continuity practices may have a head start in implementing ISO 22301 compared to those starting from scratch. The existing maturity level of the organization's business continuity practices can influence the timeline, with organizations at an early stage needing more time to build a solid foundation.

3. **Resource Availability**: The availability of resources, including personnel, budget, and technology, can impact the implementation timeline. Sufficient resources are required for activities such as policy development, risk assessment, training, documentation, and technology implementation. Limited resources may extend the timeline due to constraints on manpower and budget.

4. **Management Support and Commitment**: The level of support and commitment from top management and key stakeholders is crucial for a successful and timely implementation. Strong leadership support helps drive decision-making, allocate resources, and overcome obstacles, which can significantly impact the pace of implementation.

5. **Staff Availability and Competency**: The availability and competency of staff members involved in the implementation process can affect the timeline. Adequate staff resources should be allocated to fulfill the implementation tasks, and they should possess the necessary skills and knowledge to carry out their roles effectively.

6. **Internal Collaboration and Communication**: Effective collaboration and communication within the organization are essential for a smooth implementation process. The ability to engage stakeholders, align different departments, and coordinate activities can influence the pace at which milestones are achieved and decisions are made.

7. **Organizational Culture and Readiness**: The existing organizational culture and readiness for change can impact the implementation timeline. Organizations with a culture that embraces continuous improvement and is open to change may adapt more quickly to the requirements of ISO 22301.

8. **External Factors**: External factors such as regulatory requirements, industry-specific standards, or contractual obligations may impose additional timelines and requirements on the organization's ISO 22301 implementation.

It's important to conduct a thorough assessment of these factors to establish a realistic timeline for ISO 22301 implementation. Consider the specific circumstances of your organization, engage key stakeholders, and align expectations to ensure a successful and timely implementation process. Regular monitoring and progress tracking throughout the implementation can help identify any delays or challenges and allow for appropriate adjustments to the timeline.

6.7 Infrastructure

☐ **Identifying the necessary physical resources and infrastructure for effective BCMS**

Implementing an effective Business Continuity Management System (BCMS) requires the identification and allocation of necessary physical resources and infrastructure. These resources support the implementation, operation, and maintenance of the BCMS. Here are some key physical resources and infrastructure considerations:

1. **Facilities**: Assess the facilities needed to support the BCMS, such as office space, meeting rooms, and storage areas for documents and equipment. Consider factors like accessibility, security, and availability during emergencies. Adequate facilities help facilitate collaboration, training, and the storage of critical resources.

2. **Workstations and Equipment**: Provide appropriate workstations and equipment for employees involved in BCMS activities. This includes computers, laptops, servers, networking equipment, printers, and other necessary hardware and software. Ensure these resources are reliable, up-to-date, and properly maintained to support the efficient functioning of the BCMS.

3. **Communication Infrastructure**: Establish a reliable communication infrastructure to facilitate effective communication during normal operations and in times of crisis. This may include telephone systems, internet connectivity, email servers, messaging platforms, and emergency communication tools. Consider redundancy and backup options to ensure communication remains operational during disruptions.

4. **Power and Utilities**: Ensure a stable power supply and backup systems to minimize disruptions. Consider installing uninterruptible power supply (UPS) units, backup generators, or alternative power sources to provide continuous power in case of outages. Evaluate the availability and reliability of utilities such as water, gas, and HVAC systems to support the BCMS.

5. **Physical Security**: Implement appropriate physical security measures to protect critical resources, facilities, and data. This may involve access control systems, surveillance cameras, alarm systems, and secure storage for sensitive documents and equipment. Evaluate security measures to mitigate the risk of unauthorized access, theft, or damage.

6. **Testing and Recovery Facilities**: Identify suitable testing and recovery facilities that can be used for BCMS exercises, simulations, and recovery operations. These facilities may include alternate office spaces, recovery sites, data centers, or cloud-based services. Ensure they meet the necessary requirements for data protection, connectivity, and access to critical systems and resources.

7. **Logistical Resources**: Consider logistical resources necessary for the effective operation of the BCMS. This may include transportation arrangements for personnel during emergencies, access to suppliers and vendors for critical goods or services, and arrangements for the delivery of necessary resources or equipment.

8. **Documentation and Storage**: Allocate appropriate storage space for BCMS documentation, including policies, procedures, incident response plans, and recovery plans. Ensure proper document management systems are in place to maintain version control, access controls, and document retrieval during emergencies.

9. **Training and Exercise Facilities**: Identify suitable facilities for conducting training sessions, workshops, and BCMS exercises. These facilities should accommodate the number of participants, provide necessary equipment, and support the interactive and practical nature of the activities.

10. **Health and Safety Measures**: Ensure compliance with health and safety regulations and establish measures to protect the well-being of employees. This includes providing adequate first aid resources, emergency exits, evacuation plans, and safety equipment. Incorporate health and safety considerations into the BCMS to address potential risks and hazards.

When identifying necessary physical resources and infrastructure, consider the unique requirements and constraints of your organization. Conduct a thorough assessment, engage relevant stakeholders, and allocate resources accordingly to support the effective implementation and operation of your BCMS. Regularly review and update these resources to adapt to changing needs and emerging technologies.

Suggestions for optimizing current infrastructure

Optimizing your current infrastructure for effective implementation of a Business Continuity Management System (BCMS) involves maximizing the efficiency and functionality of existing resources. Here are some suggestions for optimizing your current infrastructure:

1. **Evaluate Current Infrastructure**: Conduct a thorough assessment of your existing infrastructure to identify strengths, weaknesses, and areas for improvement. This evaluation should include facilities, equipment, communication systems, power and utilities, physical security measures, and storage capabilities. Identify any gaps or inefficiencies that may hinder BCMS implementation.

2. **Review Physical Security Measures**: Ensure that physical security measures, such as access control systems, surveillance cameras, and alarm systems, are properly maintained and aligned with your organization's needs. Regularly assess the effectiveness of these measures, update security protocols, and address any vulnerabilities or risks identified.

3. **Enhance Communication Systems**: Review your communication infrastructure, including telephone systems, email servers, messaging platforms, and emergency communication tools. Assess the reliability and

redundancy of these systems to ensure seamless communication during normal operations and emergencies. Consider adopting cloud-based communication solutions for increased flexibility and resilience.

4. **Optimize Power and Utilities**: Evaluate your power supply and utilities infrastructure to minimize disruptions. Consider implementing uninterruptible power supply (UPS) units, backup generators, or alternative power sources to provide continuous power in case of outages. Optimize energy efficiency measures to reduce costs and environmental impact.

5. **Streamline Document Management**: Implement efficient document management systems to organize and store BCMS documentation. Utilize digital document management solutions to enhance accessibility, version control, and collaboration among stakeholders. Establish clear document retention and retrieval processes to ensure critical information is readily available when needed.

6. **Maximize Existing Equipment**: Assess the utilization and performance of your existing equipment, such as computers, servers, and networking devices. Ensure that hardware and software are up to date and capable of supporting BCMS requirements. Identify opportunities to optimize resource allocation, consolidate systems, or leverage virtualization technologies to enhance efficiency and reduce costs.

7. **Improve Data Backup and Recovery**: Review your data backup and recovery strategies to ensure data integrity and minimize downtime. Regularly test your backup systems to validate their effectiveness. Consider adopting cloud-based backup solutions or off-site storage options to enhance data redundancy and disaster recovery capabilities.

8. **Promote Remote Work Capabilities**: In light of remote work trends and the need for business continuity, evaluate your infrastructure's ability to support remote work arrangements. Assess network connectivity, security measures, and collaboration tools to enable seamless remote work during disruptions. Invest in technologies and policies that facilitate secure remote access to critical systems and data.

9. **Enhance Physical and Environmental Resilience**: Identify opportunities to improve the physical resilience of your infrastructure. This may include reinforcing buildings, implementing fire suppression systems, enhancing data center cooling, or securing critical equipment. Assess environmental risks, such as flood or seismic zones, and take appropriate mitigation measures.

10. **Regular Maintenance and Upgrades**: Implement a proactive maintenance and upgrade schedule for your infrastructure components. Regularly assess the performance, reliability, and compliance of your systems. Keep track of technology advancements and industry best practices to identify opportunities for upgrades that enhance the BCMS infrastructure.

Remember to involve key stakeholders in the optimization process, including IT personnel, facility managers, and BCMS team members. Collaboration and ongoing monitoring of your infrastructure will help identify areas for improvement and ensure that your BCMS is supported by an efficient and resilient infrastructure.

6.8 Summary

Recap of the resources required for ISO 22301 implementation

In summary, the implementation of ISO 22301 requires various resources to ensure a successful Business Continuity Management System (BCMS). Here is a recap of the resources required:

1. **Human Resources**: Skilled personnel with knowledge of ISO 22301 and business continuity practices are essential for effective implementation. This includes dedicated BCMS team members, trained employees, and management support.

2. **Technological Tools**: The appropriate technological resources, such as BCMS software, communication systems, data backup and recovery solutions, and other relevant tools, support the efficient functioning of the BCMS.

3. **Financial Resources**: Adequate financial investment is required for activities like training, consultant services, technology acquisition and maintenance, and other implementation-related costs.

4. **External Resources**: Consultants, experts, and external training programs can provide specialized knowledge and support during the ISO 22301 implementation process.

5. **Physical Resources and Infrastructure**: Facilities, workstations, equipment, communication infrastructure, power supply, physical security measures, and storage facilities are necessary for the operationalization of the BCMS.

6. **Documentation and Documentation Management**: Accurate and effective documentation, including policies, procedures, and other relevant documentation, along with appropriate document management systems, are vital for compliance with ISO 22301 requirements.

7. **Training and Awareness Programs**: Training and development initiatives ensure that employees are equipped with the necessary knowledge and skills to support the BCMS implementation.

8. **Logistical Resources**: Logistical resources, such as transportation arrangements, vendor relationships, and access to critical goods and services, are essential for maintaining business continuity during disruptive events.

9. **Health and Safety Measures**: Health and safety resources, including first aid supplies, emergency exits, and safety equipment, protect the well-being of employees and support the BCMS's ability to respond to incidents.

It is crucial to allocate and manage these resources effectively to support the implementation and operation of the BCMS. By having the right resources in place, organizations can enhance their resilience and ensure effective response and recovery during times of disruption.

Preparing for the next phase: training and awareness in BCMS

As you prepare for the next phase of training and awareness in your Business Continuity Management System (BCMS), consider the following steps:

1. **Identify Training Needs**: Assess the specific training needs within your organization related to BCMS. Determine the target audience, such as management personnel, BCMS team members, and employees in critical roles. Identify the knowledge and skills required for their respective roles in supporting the BCMS.

2. **Develop a Training Plan**: Based on the identified training needs, develop a comprehensive training plan. Outline the objectives, topics, delivery methods, and timelines for each training session. Consider a mix of training formats, such as workshops, webinars, e-learning modules, and in-person sessions, to cater to different learning preferences and logistical considerations.

3. **Select Training Resources**: Identify suitable training resources that align with your training plan. These resources may include internal subject matter experts, external trainers or consultants, training materials, industry publications, and online resources. Ensure that the selected resources are accurate, up-to-date, and relevant to ISO 22301 and business continuity practices.

4. **Tailor Training Content**: Customize the training content to address your organization's unique needs and context. Align the training material with the specific requirements of ISO 22301 and incorporate real-life scenarios and examples that resonate with your employees. Emphasize the practical application of BCMS principles and procedures to enhance understanding and engagement.

5. **Deliver Training Sessions**: Implement the training plan by conducting the identified training sessions. Ensure that the training sessions are well-organized, engaging, and interactive. Encourage participants to ask questions, share experiences, and participate in practical exercises or case studies. Use a variety of teaching methods to accommodate different learning styles and foster active participation.

6. **Promote Awareness Campaigns**: Develop awareness campaigns to educate employees about the importance of business continuity and their roles in the BCMS. Use various communication channels, such as email updates, intranet portals, posters, and newsletters, to share information about the BCMS, its objectives, and the benefits of a resilient organization. Highlight success stories or case studies to emphasize the relevance of business continuity in their daily work.

7. **Measure Training Effectiveness**: Evaluate the effectiveness of the training programs through participant feedback, assessments, and knowledge checks. Use surveys or quizzes to gauge the participants' understanding of BCMS

concepts and their confidence in applying the learned knowledge. Analyze the feedback received to identify areas for improvement and make adjustments to future training sessions.

8. **Ongoing Training and Refresher Sessions**: Ensure that training and awareness initiatives are not one-time events. Develop a plan for ongoing training and refresher sessions to reinforce knowledge, address new developments, and keep the BCMS principles and procedures top of mind for employees. Incorporate BCMS-related topics into regular employee onboarding and professional development programs.

9. **Encourage Continuous Learning**: Foster a culture of continuous learning and knowledge sharing within your organization. Encourage employees to seek additional training opportunities, attend industry conferences, and participate in webinars or workshops related to business continuity. Provide access to relevant resources and encourage employees to share their learnings and experiences to enhance collective knowledge.

10. **Monitor and Evaluate Progress**: Continuously monitor the progress and effectiveness of the training and awareness initiatives. Assess the impact of training on employees' understanding and application of BCMS principles. Regularly review and update the training plan and content to reflect changes in ISO 22301 or emerging best practices.

By implementing a robust training and awareness program, you can equip your employees with the knowledge and skills necessary to support the BCMS effectively. Building a culture of awareness and preparedness will strengthen your organization's resilience and ensure a proactive response to potential disruptions.

Throughout the chapter, there will be real-world examples, best practices, and practical tips to help organizations allocate and manage their resources effectively for successful ISO 22301 implementation.

CHAPTER 7

Training, Awareness, and Competence in BCMS

7.1 Introduction

- **Importance of training, awareness, and competence in implementing and maintaining a successful BCMS**

hapter 7 focuses on the critical aspects of training, awareness, and competence and ongoing maintenance of a BCMS.

Training and awareness programs ensure that employees at all levels of the organization understand their roles and responsibilities in relation to business continuity. These programs provide the necessary knowledge and skills to effectively respond to incidents and contribute to the overall resilience of the organization.

Competence, on the other hand, emphasizes the ability of individuals and teams to perform their designated tasks and responsibilities within the BCMS. It involves a combination of knowledge, skills, experience, and attributes required to achieve desired outcomes and effectively manage business continuity.

By addressing the importance of training, awareness, and competence, this chapter aims to guide organizations in developing comprehensive strategies to educate and empower their employees. It emphasizes the role of these factors in fostering a culture of business continuity and enhancing the organization's ability to adapt, respond, and recover from disruptive incidents.

- **Importance of training, awareness, and competence in implementing and maintaining a successful BCMS**

Importance of training, awareness, and competence in implementing and maintaining a successful BCMS

Training, awareness, and competence are vital elements in implementing and maintaining a successful Business Continuity Management System (BCMS). Here are the key reasons why they are crucial:

1. **Knowledge and Skill Development**: Training programs provide employees with the necessary knowledge and skills to effectively carry out their roles and responsibilities within the BCMS. They educate individuals about business continuity concepts, processes, and procedures, enabling them to make informed decisions and take appropriate actions during disruptive incidents.

2. **Enhanced Preparedness**: Training increases the organization's preparedness by ensuring that employees are familiar with the BCMS and its objectives. It equips them with the necessary competencies to respond swiftly and effectively in the face of disruptions, minimizing the impact on critical business operations.

3. **Improved Incident Response**: A well-trained and aware workforce is better equipped to respond to incidents promptly and efficiently. They understand their roles, know how to access resources and tools, and are familiar with incident response protocols. This enables a coordinated and effective response, reducing the time and effort required to mitigate the consequences of an incident.

4. **Cultural Shift towards Business Continuity**: Training and awareness initiatives promote a culture of business continuity within the organization. By educating employees about the importance of business continuity and their individual contributions, it fosters a sense of ownership and responsibility towards maintaining a resilient organization. This cultural shift ensures that business continuity becomes embedded in everyday operations and decision-making.

5. **Compliance with ISO 22301 Requirements**: Training and competence development are integral components of ISO 22301 compliance. The standard emphasizes the need for a competent workforce capable of implementing and maintaining the BCMS effectively. Organizations that invest in training and competence development align themselves with ISO 22301 requirements and enhance their chances of successful certification.

6. **Continuous Improvement**: Training and awareness programs facilitate ongoing learning and improvement within the organization. They provide opportunities for feedback, knowledge sharing, and identification of areas for enhancement. By continuously developing competence and awareness, organizations can adapt to changing circumstances, emerging risks, and evolving business needs.

7. **Effective Communication and Collaboration**: Training and awareness initiatives promote effective communication and collaboration among employees. They ensure that everyone understands their roles, responsibilities, and interdependencies within the BCMS. This promotes teamwork, coordination, and effective communication channels, enabling efficient information sharing and decision-making during incidents.

8. **Employee Engagement and Motivation**: Training and awareness programs demonstrate an organization's commitment to its employees' professional development and well-being. By investing in their growth, organizations foster employee engagement, satisfaction, and loyalty. Engaged employees are more likely to contribute actively to the BCMS, leveraging their knowledge and skills to improve its effectiveness.

By recognizing the importance of training, awareness, and competence, organizations can build a resilient workforce capable of effectively implementing and maintaining a

BCMS. These elements enable employees to respond to incidents, support business continuity objectives, and contribute to the overall resilience of the organization.

7.2 Building a Training Program for BCMS

Key elements of a BCMS training program

Key elements of a BCMS training program

A comprehensive BCMS training program should cover various essential elements to ensure that employees possess the necessary knowledge and skills to support business continuity within the organization. Here are key elements to consider when developing a BCMS training program:

1. **BCMS Overview**: Provide an introduction to the BCMS, including its purpose, benefits, and relevance to the organization. Explain the key concepts, components, and processes involved in business continuity management.

2. **Roles and Responsibilities**: Clearly define the roles and responsibilities of employees at different levels within the BCMS. Ensure that individuals understand their specific duties and how they contribute to the overall business continuity objectives.

3. **BCMS Policies and Procedures**: Educate employees on the BCMS policies, procedures, and guidelines. Explain the importance of adhering to these policies and provide guidance on how to implement them in their daily work.

4. **Risk Assessment and Business Impact Analysis (BIA)**: Train employees on the methodologies and tools used for risk assessment and BIA. Help them understand how to identify and evaluate risks, assess the impact on critical processes, and prioritize recovery efforts.

5. **Incident Response and Emergency Management**: Provide training on incident response protocols, including how to detect, report, and escalate incidents. Teach employees how to activate the BCMS during emergencies and guide them through the steps to mitigate, respond, and recover from disruptions.

6. **Business Continuity Plan (BCP)**: Familiarize employees with the BCP, its purpose, and its contents. Explain how to access and utilize the BCP effectively during incidents. Provide practical training on executing their specific responsibilities as outlined in the BCP.

7. **Testing and Exercising**: Train employees on the different types of BCMS tests and exercises, such as tabletop exercises, simulations, and full-scale drills. Guide them on their roles during testing, including the evaluation of response effectiveness and the identification of areas for improvement.

8. **Communication and Reporting**: Emphasize effective communication channels and protocols within the BCMS. Teach employees how to report incidents, share critical information, and disseminate updates to relevant

stakeholders. Provide guidance on maintaining accurate and timely documentation.

9. **Awareness and Culture**: Promote awareness and a culture of business continuity throughout the organization. Educate employees on the importance of their individual contributions to the BCMS and how they can actively participate in enhancing organizational resilience.

10. **Training Evaluation and Refresher Programs**: Establish mechanisms to evaluate the effectiveness of the training program, such as assessments, quizzes, or practical evaluations. Offer refresher courses periodically to reinforce knowledge, address new developments, and ensure ongoing competence.

11. **Integration with Other Training Initiatives**: Integrate BCMS training with existing training programs and initiatives in the organization. Ensure alignment with other management system standards, such as quality or environmental management systems, to leverage synergies and optimize resources.

Remember to tailor the training program to the specific needs and context of your organization. Use a variety of training methods, such as instructor-led sessions, e-learning modules, workshops, and hands-on exercises, to accommodate different learning styles and preferences. Continuously assess and update the training program to reflect changes in the BCMS, industry best practices, and emerging risks.

How to design and deliver effective BCMS training

Designing and delivering effective BCMS training requires careful planning and consideration of various factors. Here are some steps to guide you in designing and delivering impactful BCMS training:

1. **Identify Training Objectives**: Clarify the specific objectives of the training program. Determine what knowledge and skills participants should gain from the training and how it aligns with the overall goals of the BCMS.

2. **Analyze Training Needs**: Conduct a thorough analysis of the training needs within your organization. Identify the target audience, their current knowledge level, and the specific areas where training is required. Consider the roles and responsibilities of different employees and their involvement in the BCMS.

3. **Develop a Training Plan**: Based on the training objectives and needs analysis, create a comprehensive training plan. Outline the topics, training methods, duration, and resources required for each training session. Consider the most effective delivery methods, such as in-person workshops, e-learning modules, or a combination of both.

4. **Engage Subject Matter Experts**: Work closely with subject matter experts (SMEs) to develop the training content. SMEs can provide valuable insights, practical examples, and real-world scenarios to enhance the relevance and credibility of the training material.

5. **Structure the Training Content**: Organize the training content in a logical and sequential manner. Start with foundational concepts before progressing to more advanced topics. Use clear and concise language, avoiding jargon or technical terms that may be unfamiliar to participants.

6. **Utilize Interactive Training Techniques**: Incorporate interactive training techniques to engage participants and promote active learning. Include case studies, group discussions, role plays, and hands-on exercises to encourage participation and practical application of concepts.

7. **Provide Real-World Examples**: Use real-world examples and case studies relevant to your organization's industry or sector. This helps participants understand how the BCMS principles and procedures apply in practical scenarios and reinforces the importance of business continuity.

8. **Balance Theory and Practical Application**: Strike a balance between theoretical knowledge and practical application. Provide participants with opportunities to apply their learning through simulations, exercises, or scenario-based assessments. This allows them to practice problem-solving, decision-making, and response coordination within the BCMS context.

9. **Use Visual Aids and Multimedia**: Incorporate visual aids, such as slides, infographics, or videos, to enhance understanding and retention of information. Visuals can simplify complex concepts, make the training more engaging, and facilitate better knowledge retention.

10. **Provide Job-Specific Training**: Tailor the training content to address the specific roles and responsibilities of participants within the BCMS. Customize examples and case studies to reflect their job functions, enabling them to directly apply the knowledge gained.

11. **Offer Post-Training Support**: Provide post-training support to reinforce learning and address any questions or concerns that participants may have. This can include access to additional resources, a dedicated helpline, or ongoing communication channels for knowledge sharing.

12. **Evaluate Training Effectiveness**: Assess the effectiveness of the training program through participant feedback, assessments, or quizzes. Use the feedback to identify areas for improvement and make necessary adjustments to future training sessions.

13. **Continuously Improve the Training Program**: Regularly review and update the training program to incorporate new industry developments, changes in the BCMS, or emerging best practices. Seek feedback from participants, trainers, and BCMS stakeholders to ensure the program remains relevant and impactful.

Remember that effective BCMS training is an ongoing process. Plan for regular refresher training sessions to reinforce knowledge, address updates, and ensure continued competence within the organization. By designing and delivering effective BCMS training, you can enhance the skills, awareness, and commitment of your workforce to support the successful implementation and maintenance of the BCMS.

7.3 Cultivating Awareness about BCMS

Strategies for creating BCMS awareness throughout the organization

Creating BCMS awareness throughout the organization is essential to foster a culture of business continuity and ensure that employees understand the importance of their roles in supporting the BCMS. Here are some strategies to effectively promote BCMS awareness:

1. **Communication Plan**: Develop a comprehensive communication plan specifically for BCMS awareness. Outline the key messages, target audience, communication channels, and frequency of communication. Ensure that the plan encompasses all levels of the organization, from top management to front-line employees.

2. **Top-Down Communication**: Begin by establishing leadership support and commitment to the BCMS. Encourage top management to communicate the importance of business continuity and their commitment to its success. This can be done through company-wide emails, town hall meetings, or video messages.

3. **Training and Workshops**: Conduct regular training sessions and workshops to educate employees about business continuity concepts, their roles and responsibilities, and the BCMS's overall objectives. These sessions can be conducted in person, through webinars, or e-learning modules. Make the training interactive and engaging to encourage participation and knowledge retention.

4. **Awareness Campaigns**: Launch targeted awareness campaigns to highlight the significance of business continuity. Use posters, infographics, newsletters, and internal company publications to reinforce key messages. Promote success stories, case studies, and real-world examples to illustrate the value of business continuity in protecting the organization.

5. **Internal Communication Channels**: Utilize existing internal communication channels, such as intranet portals, email newsletters, digital signage, or company-wide meetings, to share BCMS updates, achievements, and reminders. Create dedicated sections or pages on the intranet to provide easy access to BCMS-related resources, documentation, and training materials.

6. **Business Continuity Champions**: Identify and engage BCMS champions within different departments or teams. These champions can serve as advocates for business continuity, promoting awareness, answering questions, and encouraging active participation. Provide them with additional training and resources to support their role effectively.

7. **Simulation Exercises**: Conduct regular simulation exercises, such as tabletop exercises or scenario-based simulations, to demonstrate the practical application of the BCMS. These exercises allow employees to practice their

response and decision-making skills in a controlled environment, fostering better understanding and preparedness.

8. **Reward and Recognition**: Recognize and reward employees who actively contribute to the BCMS. This can be through formal recognition programs, certificates of appreciation, or public acknowledgment of their efforts. Celebrate achievements and milestones to reinforce a positive BCMS culture.

9. **Incorporate BCMS in Onboarding**: Integrate BCMS awareness into the onboarding process for new employees. Provide them with an overview of the BCMS, its importance, and their role within it. This ensures that business continuity becomes ingrained in their understanding of the organization from the beginning.

10. **Continuous Education and Refreshers**: Offer ongoing education and refresher sessions to keep BCMS awareness alive. This can include regular updates on emerging risks, changes in procedures, or industry best practices. Leverage internal and external subject matter experts to provide specialized training and insights.

11. **Collaboration and Cross-Functional Involvement**: Encourage cross-functional collaboration and involvement in BCMS activities. Foster communication and cooperation between departments to ensure a unified approach to business continuity. This promotes a shared understanding of the BCMS and its goals.

12. **Feedback and Surveys**: Regularly seek feedback from employees regarding their understanding and perception of the BCMS. Conduct surveys or focus groups to gauge awareness levels, identify areas for improvement, and gather suggestions. Actively address any concerns or misconceptions to enhance engagement and alignment.

Tools and techniques for disseminating BCMS information

Disseminating BCMS information effectively requires the use of various tools and techniques to ensure that the information reaches the intended audience and is easily understood. Here are some tools and techniques for disseminating BCMS information:

1. **Email Communications**: Use email as a primary communication tool to distribute BCMS updates, announcements, and reminders. Ensure that the emails are concise, clear, and targeted to the appropriate recipients. Include relevant links or attachments for further information.

2. **Intranet Portals**: Utilize the organization's intranet portal to create dedicated BCMS sections or pages. This serves as a central repository for BCMS-related documents, policies, procedures, training materials, and frequently asked questions (FAQs). Ensure that the information is well-organized, easily accessible, and regularly updated.

3. **Newsletters**: Include BCMS-related updates, success stories, and tips in regular newsletters circulated within the organization. Keep the content

concise, engaging, and visually appealing to capture employees' attention and encourage them to read and retain the information.

4. **Digital Signage**: Display BCMS-related messages, infographics, or reminders on digital signage screens located in common areas, such as break rooms, cafeterias, or lobbies. This grabs employees' attention and reinforces BCMS messages in a visually impactful manner.

5. **Posters and Infographics**: Create visually appealing posters and infographics that summarize key BCMS concepts, procedures, or emergency response protocols. Display them in prominent locations throughout the organization to raise awareness and provide quick reference points.

6. **Training Materials**: Develop comprehensive training materials, such as slide decks, handouts, and participant guides, to support BCMS training sessions. Ensure that the materials are well-structured, visually appealing, and aligned with the training objectives. Provide practical examples and case studies to enhance understanding.

7. **Webinars and E-Learning Modules**: Conduct webinars or develop interactive e-learning modules to deliver BCMS training remotely. These platforms allow employees to learn at their own pace and provide flexibility in accessing training materials. Incorporate quizzes or assessments to reinforce learning and measure comprehension.

8. **Videos and Podcasts**: Create short educational videos or podcasts that explain BCMS concepts, provide guidance on procedures, or share real-life scenarios. Use engaging visuals, animations, or interviews with subject matter experts to make the content more engaging and memorable.

9. **Workshops and Presentations**: Conduct in-person or virtual workshops and presentations to deliver BCMS information and facilitate interactive discussions. Encourage participation, ask for feedback, and address questions or concerns raised by participants.

10. **One-on-One Meetings and Team Briefings**: Schedule one-on-one meetings or team briefings with key stakeholders, department heads, or managers to discuss BCMS updates, objectives, and individual responsibilities. This provides an opportunity for personalized communication, addressing specific concerns, and fostering engagement.

11. **Social Media and Collaboration Platforms**: Leverage social media platforms or internal collaboration tools to share BCMS information. Create dedicated groups or channels where employees can discuss BCMS topics, ask questions, and share best practices. Encourage employees to engage and participate actively in these platforms.

12. **Town Hall Meetings and All-Hands Sessions**: Organize town hall meetings or all-hands sessions where BCMS-related updates and initiatives are shared by top management or BCMS leaders. These sessions allow for direct communication, open dialogue, and the opportunity to address any concerns or misconceptions.

Remember to use a combination of these tools and techniques to cater to different communication preferences and learning styles within your organization. Regularly assess the effectiveness of your communication methods and make adjustments as needed to ensure that BCMS information is disseminated effectively and understood by employees.

7.4 Developing Competence in BCMS

▫Understanding the concept of competence in the context of BCMS

In the context of a Business Continuity Management System (BCMS), competence refers to the knowledge, skills, abilities, and attributes that individuals or teams possess to perform their roles effectively within the BCMS framework. Competence goes beyond mere qualifications or experience and encompasses the capacity to apply knowledge and skills in practical scenarios related to business continuity.

Competence is essential within a BCMS as it ensures that individuals have the necessary capabilities to contribute to the development, implementation, and maintenance of the system. It enables them to fulfill their responsibilities, make informed decisions, and carry out their assigned tasks with confidence.

Competence in the context of BCMS can include the following aspects:

1. **Knowledge**: Competence requires individuals to have a deep understanding of business continuity concepts, principles, and best practices. They should be familiar with industry standards, regulations, and guidelines relevant to business continuity management.

2. **Skills**: Competence involves possessing the practical skills necessary to perform specific tasks related to business continuity. These skills may include conducting risk assessments, developing business impact analyses (BIA), creating business continuity plans (BCP), implementing incident response procedures, or facilitating recovery exercises.

3. **Experience**: Competence is often developed and refined through practical experience. Individuals who have successfully participated in incident response activities, contributed to BCP development, or engaged in recovery exercises are likely to have a higher level of competence in their respective roles.

4. **Attributes**: Certain personal attributes contribute to competence in BCMS, such as effective communication, problem-solving abilities, adaptability, and attention to detail. These attributes enable individuals to navigate complex situations, collaborate with stakeholders, and make sound decisions during business continuity incidents.

5. **Continuous Learning**: Competence requires individuals to engage in ongoing learning and professional development to stay abreast of industry trends, emerging risks, and evolving best practices in business continuity. Continuous learning ensures that individuals remain competent and adaptable in a rapidly changing environment.

It is important for organizations to assess and ensure the competence of their employees involved in the BCMS. This can be done through a combination of methods such as training programs, certifications, assessments, on-the-job evaluations, and performance reviews. By promoting competence, organizations can enhance the effectiveness of their BCMS and improve their overall resilience in the face of disruptive incidents.

Steps to identify the necessary competencies and develop them within the organization

Identifying the necessary competencies and developing them within the organization is crucial for ensuring the effectiveness of the Business Continuity Management System (BCMS). Here are the steps to help you identify and develop the required competencies:

1. **Define Roles and Responsibilities**: Start by clearly defining the roles and responsibilities within the BCMS. Identify the key positions and functions that contribute to the BCMS implementation and maintenance, such as BCMS manager, risk assessment coordinator, BIA analyst, incident response team leader, etc.

2. **Conduct a Competency Gap Analysis**: Perform a competency gap analysis to assess the existing competencies of individuals in relation to the required competencies for their respective roles. Identify the gaps between the current skills, knowledge, and attributes of employees and the desired competencies needed for the successful implementation of the BCMS.

3. **Establish Competency Framework**: Develop a competency framework that outlines the desired competencies for each role within the BCMS. This framework should clearly define the knowledge, skills, experience, and attributes necessary for individuals to fulfill their responsibilities effectively.

4. **Identify Training and Development Needs**: Based on the competency gap analysis and the established competency framework, identify the specific training and development needs for each role. Determine the areas where individuals require additional knowledge, skills, or experience to bridge the competency gaps.

5. **Design Training Programs**: Design and implement training programs tailored to address the identified training and development needs. These programs can include formal training sessions, workshops, e-learning modules, on-the-job training, mentorship programs, or participation in industry conferences and seminars. Ensure that the training programs cover the necessary technical knowledge, practical skills, and relevant industry standards.

6. **Provide Ongoing Learning Opportunities**: Foster a culture of continuous learning and professional development within the organization. Encourage employees to participate in webinars, conferences, and workshops related to business continuity and provide them with resources, such as industry publications or online learning platforms, to expand their knowledge and skills continuously.

7. **Support Certification and Professional Development**: Encourage employees to pursue relevant certifications in business continuity management, risk management, or related disciplines. Support their efforts by providing resources, study materials, and financial assistance for certification exams. Acknowledge and recognize employees who achieve certifications or demonstrate exceptional competence in their roles.

8. **Promote Cross-Functional Collaboration**: Facilitate cross-functional collaboration and knowledge sharing among employees involved in the BCMS. Encourage team members to work together, share best practices, and learn from each other's experiences. This helps to build a collective competence and a stronger BCMS culture within the organization.

9. **Measure and Evaluate Competence**: Implement mechanisms to assess and evaluate the competence of individuals within the BCMS. This can include performance evaluations, knowledge assessments, practical simulations, or competency-based interviews. Regularly review and update the competency framework and training programs based on the feedback and performance results.

10. **Provide Support and Resources**: Ensure that employees have access to the necessary resources, tools, and support systems to enhance their competence. This includes providing access to relevant documentation, technology platforms, and subject matter experts who can provide guidance and mentorship.

By following these steps, organizations can systematically identify the necessary competencies, bridge any competency gaps, and develop a skilled and capable workforce to support the successful implementation and maintenance of the BCMS. Continuous evaluation and improvement of competencies will help organizations adapt to changing circumstances, emerging risks, and evolving business continuity needs.

7.5 Role of Leadership in BCMS Training and Awareness

The critical role of top management in fostering a culture of learning and awareness

Top management plays a critical role in fostering a culture of learning and awareness within an organization. Their commitment and actions set the tone for the entire workforce and influence the importance placed on continuous learning and awareness. Here are key ways in which top management can foster a culture of learning and awareness:

1. **Lead by Example**: Top management should actively demonstrate their commitment to learning and awareness by participating in training programs, attending workshops, and engaging in continuous professional development. When employees see leaders prioritizing learning, they are more likely to follow suit.

2. **Promote a Learning Mindset**: Encourage a growth mindset where employees are open to learning, embracing new challenges, and seeking opportunities for development. Top management should emphasize the value of learning and demonstrate that it is an ongoing process, not limited to formal training sessions.

3. **Allocate Resources**: Provide the necessary resources, such as time, budget, and tools, to support employee learning and awareness initiatives. This includes funding for training programs, access to relevant learning materials and technologies, and opportunities to attend conferences or workshops.

4. **Incorporate Learning in Performance Management**: Integrate learning and development goals into the performance management process. Set clear expectations for employees to engage in continuous learning and tie it to their performance evaluations and career growth opportunities.

5. **Communicate the Importance of Learning**: Top management should consistently communicate the importance of learning and awareness in achieving business objectives and maintaining a competitive edge. Emphasize how continuous learning contributes to individual and organizational success, resilience, and adaptability.

6. **Provide Learning Opportunities**: Offer a variety of learning opportunities to cater to different learning styles and preferences. This can include in-person or virtual training sessions, e-learning modules, webinars, workshops, mentorship programs, or cross-functional projects. Encourage employees to take advantage of these opportunities and support them in their learning journey.

7. **Create a Safe Learning Environment**: Foster an environment where employees feel safe to ask questions, share ideas, and learn from mistakes. Encourage open communication, provide constructive feedback, and create forums for knowledge sharing and collaboration.

8. **Recognize and Reward Learning Efforts**: Acknowledge and reward employees who actively engage in learning and demonstrate their enhanced skills or knowledge. This can be through public recognition, career advancement opportunities, or incentives tied to professional development achievements.

9. **Integrate Learning into Business Processes**: Embed learning and awareness initiatives into existing business processes and workflows. For example, incorporate brief training sessions or knowledge sharing discussions into team meetings or project kick-offs. This reinforces the importance of learning and makes it an integral part of daily operations.

10. **Measure Learning Outcomes**: Establish mechanisms to measure the impact and effectiveness of learning initiatives. Gather feedback from employees, conduct assessments or quizzes to evaluate knowledge retention, and monitor the application of newly acquired skills in real-life scenarios. Use this data to continuously improve learning programs.

By actively promoting and supporting a culture of learning and awareness, top management sets the foundation for a workforce that is engaged, adaptable, and continuously striving for improvement. This, in turn, enhances the organization's ability to effectively implement and maintain the BCMS and respond to business continuity challenges.

Tips for leaders to drive BCMS training and awareness initiatives

Driving BCMS training and awareness initiatives requires strong leadership and active engagement from organizational leaders. Here are some tips for leaders to effectively drive BCMS training and awareness initiatives:

1. **Lead by Example**: Actively participate in BCMS training programs and demonstrate your commitment to continuous learning and awareness. This sets a powerful example for employees and shows that training and awareness are a priority for leadership.

2. **Communicate the Importance**: Clearly communicate the significance of BCMS training and awareness to the organization's overall resilience and success. Emphasize the role that each employee plays in maintaining business continuity and highlight the potential impact of their actions on the organization and its stakeholders.

3. **Align with Business Objectives**: Connect BCMS training and awareness initiatives with the organization's strategic goals. Show how a well-informed and prepared workforce contributes to achieving those objectives, minimizing disruptions, and protecting the organization's reputation and operations.

4. **Provide Resources and Support**: Ensure that employees have access to the necessary resources, tools, and support systems for BCMS training and awareness. Allocate budgets for training programs, provide relevant learning materials, and offer guidance or mentorship to those who need it.

5. **Set Expectations**: Clearly communicate your expectations regarding BCMS training and awareness to employees. Incorporate these expectations into performance goals and evaluations to emphasize their importance. Regularly discuss progress and provide feedback to encourage continuous improvement.

6. **Promote Cross-Functional Collaboration**: Foster collaboration and knowledge sharing across departments and teams. Encourage employees to share their experiences, lessons learned, and best practices related to BCMS training and awareness. Create forums or platforms for employees to engage in discussions and exchange ideas.

7. **Empower BCMS Champions**: Identify BCMS champions within the organization who can serve as ambassadors for training and awareness. Empower them to lead initiatives, share their expertise, and promote a culture of learning. Recognize and reward their efforts to further motivate others.

8. **Tailor Training to Roles**: Recognize that different roles within the organization have varying training needs. Customize training programs to align with specific job functions and responsibilities. Ensure that employees

understand how BCMS principles apply to their individual roles and empower them to fulfill their responsibilities effectively.

9. **Provide Regular Updates and Reminders**: Regularly communicate BCMS updates, reminders, and relevant information to employees. Use multiple communication channels, such as email, intranet portals, newsletters, or team meetings, to keep employees informed and engaged in BCMS-related activities.

10. **Monitor and Evaluate Progress**: Continuously monitor the effectiveness of BCMS training and awareness initiatives. Gather feedback from employees, track participation rates, assess knowledge retention, and evaluate the application of learned skills. Use this feedback to refine and improve the training programs over time.

By following these tips, leaders can effectively drive BCMS training and awareness initiatives, cultivate a culture of preparedness and resilience, and ensure that employees are equipped with the knowledge and skills to contribute to the organization's business continuity efforts.

7.6 Evaluating BCMS Training and Competence Development

- Importance of assessing the effectiveness of BCMS training and competence development

Assessing the effectiveness of BCMS training and competence development is crucial for several reasons:

1. **Quality Assurance**: Assessments help ensure that the training and competence development programs meet the desired standards of quality and effectiveness. It allows organizations to evaluate whether the intended learning outcomes are being achieved and if employees are acquiring the necessary knowledge, skills, and competencies.

2. **Identifying Gaps and Improvements**: Assessments provide insights into areas where employees may be lacking in competence or where training programs may need improvement. By identifying these gaps, organizations can take appropriate measures to address them, such as offering additional training or modifying the existing programs to enhance their effectiveness.

3. **Validation of Training Investments**: Assessing the effectiveness of BCMS training and competence development helps organizations validate their investment in these initiatives. It allows them to gauge the return on investment by determining if the training has resulted in improved skills, increased employee engagement, better decision-making, or enhanced performance in business continuity-related tasks.

4. **Continuous Improvement**: Regular assessments foster a culture of continuous improvement. They enable organizations to identify trends, patterns, and areas of improvement over time. By consistently evaluating the

effectiveness of training programs, organizations can make informed decisions to enhance their training strategies, methodologies, and resources.

5. **Adaptation to Changing Needs**: Assessments help organizations adapt their BCMS training and competence development initiatives to meet evolving needs. As business continuity requirements, industry standards, or regulatory frameworks change, organizations can assess whether their training programs align with these changes and update them accordingly to ensure ongoing relevance and compliance.

6. **Risk Mitigation**: Effective training and competence development contribute to risk mitigation by ensuring that employees are equipped with the necessary skills and knowledge to respond effectively to business continuity incidents. Assessments provide insights into areas of improvement, allowing organizations to minimize risks associated with human error or inadequate competence.

7. **Employee Engagement and Satisfaction**: Assessing the effectiveness of training and competence development programs demonstrates a commitment to employee growth and development. It enhances employee engagement and job satisfaction by providing opportunities for skill enhancement and career advancement. Regular assessments also show employees that their competence development is valued and their progress is recognized.

8. **Compliance Requirements**: Some industry regulations or standards may require organizations to assess the effectiveness of their BCMS training and competence development initiatives. By conducting assessments, organizations can demonstrate compliance with these requirements and provide evidence of their commitment to ongoing improvement.

To assess the effectiveness of BCMS training and competence development, organizations can use various methods such as knowledge assessments, skills evaluations, performance evaluations, feedback surveys, simulations, and observations. It is important to establish clear assessment criteria, measure the desired learning outcomes, and gather feedback from participants and stakeholders. The assessment findings should be used to drive continuous improvement and ensure that the training and competence development programs align with organizational goals and the evolving needs of the BCMS.

▢ Methods and tools for evaluation

When evaluating the effectiveness of BCMS training and competence development, organizations can utilize various methods and tools to gather data and assess the outcomes. Here are some commonly used methods and tools for evaluation:

1. **Knowledge Assessments**: Conduct quizzes, tests, or exams to evaluate the participants' understanding of BCMS concepts, procedures, and best practices. Knowledge assessments can be in the form of multiple-choice questions, case studies, or scenario-based assessments.

2. **Skills Demonstrations**: Have participants demonstrate their skills and competencies related to BCMS through practical exercises, simulations, or

role-playing scenarios. This allows for the observation and evaluation of their application of knowledge in real or simulated situations.

3. **Performance Evaluations**: Assess participants' performance in BCMS-related tasks and responsibilities through performance evaluations. This can involve supervisor assessments, peer reviews, or self-assessments to gauge how effectively individuals are applying their knowledge and skills in practical scenarios.

4. **Observations**: Observe participants in action during BCMS-related activities, such as training exercises, incident response simulations, or recovery exercises. This allows for direct observation of their behavior, decision-making, and adherence to established processes and procedures.

5. **Feedback Surveys**: Collect feedback from participants through anonymous surveys or questionnaires. These surveys can include questions about the relevance, effectiveness, and usefulness of the training or competence development activities. Feedback surveys provide insights into participants' perceptions, satisfaction levels, and suggestions for improvement.

6. **Focus Groups or Interviews**: Conduct focus group discussions or individual interviews with participants to gather qualitative feedback on their experiences with BCMS training and competence development. This allows for in-depth exploration of participants' perspectives, insights, and suggestions for improvement.

7. **Performance Metrics**: Define key performance indicators (KPIs) related to BCMS implementation and evaluate the impact of training and competence development initiatives on those metrics. This can include metrics such as incident response time, recovery time objectives, or the successful completion of recovery exercises.

8. **Case Studies and Success Stories**: Collect and analyze case studies or success stories that demonstrate how individuals or teams have applied their training and competence development to real-life situations. These case studies provide evidence of the practical impact of the training and competence development initiatives.

9. **Mentorship and Coaching**: Engage in one-on-one mentorship or coaching sessions with individuals or teams to provide personalized guidance and support. These sessions allow for the assessment of progress, identification of areas for improvement, and the provision of targeted feedback.

10. **Benchmarking and External Validation**: Compare the organization's training and competence development efforts with industry best practices or benchmarks. This can involve seeking external validation through certifications, external audits, or peer assessments.

It's important to use a combination of these evaluation methods and tools to gather comprehensive data and assess the effectiveness of BCMS training and competence development initiatives. The data collected should be analyzed, and the findings should be used to inform decision-making, identify areas for improvement, and drive continuous enhancement of the training and competence development programs.

7.7 Continual Improvement of BCMS Training and Competence

☐ Need for ongoing refinement of BCMS training and competence development activities

Ongoing refinement of BCMS training and competence development activities is essential for several reasons:

1. **Evolution of Business Continuity Landscape**: The business continuity landscape is dynamic, with emerging risks, evolving regulations, and changing industry practices. Ongoing refinement ensures that BCMS training and competence development activities stay up to date and aligned with the latest developments, ensuring the organization's ability to address new challenges effectively.

2. **Continuous Improvement**: Regular refinement allows organizations to identify areas for improvement in their training and competence development activities. By collecting feedback, evaluating outcomes, and analyzing performance data, organizations can make informed decisions to enhance the effectiveness, relevance, and efficiency of their programs.

3. **Employee Growth and Development**: Ongoing refinement supports the growth and development of employees. As individuals acquire new skills, knowledge, and competencies, it becomes necessary to update and refine the training and competence development activities to meet their changing needs and foster their continued professional growth.

4. **Feedback and Lessons Learned**: Continuous refinement provides an opportunity to incorporate feedback and lessons learned from previous training and competence development initiatives. This feedback can come from participants, trainers, supervisors, or other stakeholders involved in the BCMS. By incorporating feedback, organizations can address any identified gaps or areas of improvement in subsequent activities.

5. **Adaptation to Organizational Changes**: Organizations undergo changes such as restructuring, technological advancements, or expansion into new markets. Ongoing refinement ensures that BCMS training and competence development activities are aligned with these organizational changes, reflecting the current roles, responsibilities, and business processes within the organization.

6. **Emerging Learning Methods and Technologies**: Learning methods and technologies continually evolve, offering new opportunities to enhance training and competence development. Ongoing refinement allows organizations to explore and incorporate emerging learning methods, such as microlearning, gamification, or virtual reality, to make the training more engaging, interactive, and effective.

7. **Compliance with Standards and Regulations**: Compliance requirements for business continuity management may change over time.

Ongoing refinement ensures that BCMS training and competence development activities remain compliant with the relevant standards and regulations. This helps organizations demonstrate their commitment to maintaining compliance and continuously improving their BCMS.

8. **Engagement and Motivation**: Regular refinement of training and competence development activities keeps participants engaged and motivated. By introducing new approaches, content, or delivery methods, organizations can maintain participants' interest and enthusiasm, leading to better learning outcomes and application of acquired skills in real-world scenarios.

9. **Continuous Alignment with Business Objectives**: Business objectives and priorities may shift over time. Ongoing refinement ensures that BCMS training and competence development activities remain aligned with the current business objectives, allowing participants to acquire the skills and knowledge required to contribute effectively to the organization's strategic goals.

10. **Competitive Advantage**: Organizations that consistently refine their BCMS training and competence development activities gain a competitive edge. By staying ahead of industry trends and best practices, organizations can build a workforce that is better prepared, more competent, and capable of effectively managing business continuity incidents. This enhances their resilience and positions them as leaders in their respective industries.

By recognizing the need for ongoing refinement, organizations can continually enhance the quality, relevance, and effectiveness of their BCMS training and competence development activities. This iterative process ensures that training programs remain current, engaging, and aligned with the organization's evolving needs and objectives.

Approaches for continual improvement

Continual improvement is a fundamental principle of ISO 22301 and involves the ongoing enhancement of the Business Continuity Management System (BCMS) to achieve better performance and outcomes. Here are some approaches for continual improvement:

1. **Establish a Culture of Continuous Improvement**: Foster a culture where continuous improvement is embraced at all levels of the organization. Encourage employees to share ideas, suggestions, and lessons learned from incidents or exercises. Create channels for open communication and provide recognition for individuals or teams that contribute to improvement initiatives.

2. **Regularly Monitor Key Performance Indicators (KPIs)**: Define and track key performance indicators related to business continuity management. Continuously monitor and analyze these KPIs to identify areas for improvement. Examples of relevant KPIs include recovery time objectives, incident response effectiveness, or the number of business continuity exercises conducted.

3. **Collect and Analyze Data**: Gather data from various sources, such as incident reports, exercise evaluations, or feedback surveys, to identify trends, patterns, and areas of improvement. Analyze the data to gain insights into the effectiveness of the BCMS and identify areas that require attention.

4. **Perform Internal Audits**: Conduct regular internal audits to assess the compliance, effectiveness, and efficiency of the BCMS. Internal audits help identify gaps, non-conformities, and areas for improvement. Use the findings from audits as a basis for implementing corrective actions and enhancing the BCMS.

5. **Encourage Lessons Learned and After-Action Reviews**: Encourage the documentation and sharing of lessons learned from incidents, exercises, or actual business disruptions. Conduct after-action reviews to evaluate the effectiveness of the response and identify areas that need improvement. Implement the identified improvements in subsequent training, procedures, or recovery plans.

6. **Engage Stakeholders**: Involve relevant stakeholders, such as employees, customers, suppliers, or external experts, in the improvement process. Seek their input, feedback, and suggestions for enhancing the BCMS. Collaboration and diverse perspectives can lead to innovative solutions and more robust improvements.

7. **Benchmarking**: Compare the organization's BCMS practices, performance, and outcomes with industry benchmarks or best practices. Benchmarking allows organizations to identify areas of strength and areas for improvement. Learn from industry leaders and adapt their successful strategies to enhance the BCMS.

8. **Continuously Update Policies, Procedures, and Documentation**: Regularly review and update BCMS policies, procedures, and documentation to reflect evolving best practices, regulatory requirements, or lessons learned. Ensure that the documentation remains current, accurate, and accessible to relevant stakeholders.

9. **Provide Training and Professional Development**: Invest in training programs and professional development opportunities for employees involved in BCMS implementation and maintenance. Equip them with the necessary skills and knowledge to identify improvement opportunities, implement changes, and drive continual improvement efforts.

10. **Set Improvement Goals**: Establish specific improvement goals and objectives for the BCMS. These goals should be measurable and time-bound, providing a clear direction for improvement efforts. Regularly review progress against these goals and adjust strategies as needed.

By adopting these approaches, organizations can foster a culture of continual improvement, systematically identify areas for enhancement, and ensure that the BCMS remains robust, effective, and aligned with business objectives. Continual improvement helps organizations adapt to changing circumstances, address emerging risks, and continuously enhance their business continuity capabilities.

7.8 Summary

Recap of the importance of training, awareness, and competence in BCMS

Chapter 7 focused on the importance of training, awareness, and competence in the successful implementation and maintenance of a Business Continuity Management System (BCMS). Here is a recap of the key points covered:

1. **Importance of Training, Awareness, and Competence**: Training equips employees with the knowledge and skills necessary to effectively respond to business continuity incidents. Awareness ensures that individuals understand their roles and responsibilities within the BCMS. Competence ensures that employees possess the necessary abilities to carry out their tasks successfully.

2. **Key Elements of a BCMS Training Program**: A comprehensive BCMS training program includes an understanding of BCMS principles, processes, procedures, incident response protocols, recovery techniques, and relevant regulations or standards. It should be tailored to different roles and responsibilities within the organization.

3. **Designing and Delivering Effective BCMS Training**: Effective BCMS training involves understanding the target audience, setting clear objectives, selecting appropriate training methods, developing relevant content, utilizing interactive and engaging techniques, and evaluating the effectiveness of the training program.

4. **Strategies for Creating BCMS Awareness**: BCMS awareness initiatives should aim to communicate the purpose and importance of the BCMS, the roles and responsibilities of employees, the potential impact of incidents, and the benefits of business continuity planning. Communication channels, such as emails, intranet portals, newsletters, and team meetings, should be utilized effectively.

5. **Tools and Techniques for Disseminating BCMS Information**: Various tools and techniques can be used to disseminate BCMS information, including presentations, videos, posters, online platforms, workshops, and webinars. These tools should be accessible, engaging, and tailored to the audience's needs.

6. **Understanding Competence in the Context of BCMS**: Competence refers to the combination of knowledge, skills, experience, and attributes necessary to perform specific tasks or roles within the BCMS. It includes both technical and behavioral competencies that contribute to effective business continuity management.

7. **Steps to Identify and Develop Competencies**: Identifying the necessary competencies involves assessing the requirements of each role within the BCMS, determining the existing competencies, and identifying any gaps.

Development can be achieved through training, mentoring, on-the-job experiences, and professional development opportunities.

8. **The Role of Top Management in Driving Training and Awareness Initiatives**: Top management plays a crucial role in supporting and driving BCMS training and awareness initiatives. Their commitment, resources allocation, and active participation set the tone for the organization's overall commitment to business continuity.

By emphasizing the importance of training, awareness, and competence, organizations can ensure that their workforce is equipped with the necessary knowledge and skills to effectively respond to business continuity incidents. Continuous training, awareness initiatives, and competence development contribute to a strong BCMS and enhance the organization's resilience in the face of disruptions.

Gearing up for the next step: internal audit and management review

- Chapter 8: Internal Audit and Management Review 8.1 Introduction • The role of internal audit and management review in the ISO 22301 implementation process • Importance of evaluating the effectiveness of the BCMS

- 8.2 Internal Audit Process • Overview of the internal audit process in ISO 22301 • Defining the scope and objectives of the internal audit • Planning and conducting internal audits • Evaluating and documenting audit findings • Preparing audit reports and follow-up actions

- 8.3 Management Review Process • Importance of management review in maintaining the effectiveness of the BCMS • Defining the scope and objectives of the management review • Scheduling and conducting management review meetings • Evaluating the performance of the BCMS against objectives and targets • Reviewing audit findings, corrective actions, and continual improvement initiatives • Documenting management review outcomes and decisions

- 8.4 Roles and Responsibilities in Internal Audit and Management Review • The role of the internal audit team and management representatives • Responsibilities of top management in the internal audit and management review processes • Collaboration between internal audit, management, and other relevant stakeholders

- 8.5 Continual Improvement Based on Audit Findings and Management Review • Utilizing audit findings and management review outcomes to drive continual improvement • Identifying areas for corrective actions and preventive measures • Implementing changes and evaluating their effectiveness • Tracking progress and monitoring the impact of improvement initiatives

- 8.6 Integration of Internal Audit and Management Review with Other Management Systems • Integration of ISO 22301 internal audit and management review processes with other ISO management system standards •

Benefits and synergies of integrating audit and review activities across multiple management systems

☐ 8.7 Auditing and Reviewing External Providers • Considerations for auditing and reviewing external providers of critical products or services • Assessing the resilience and continuity capabilities of external providers • Evaluating the effectiveness of contractual arrangements and service level agreements

☐ 8.8 Summary • Recap of the internal audit and management review processes and their significance in evaluating and improving the BCMS

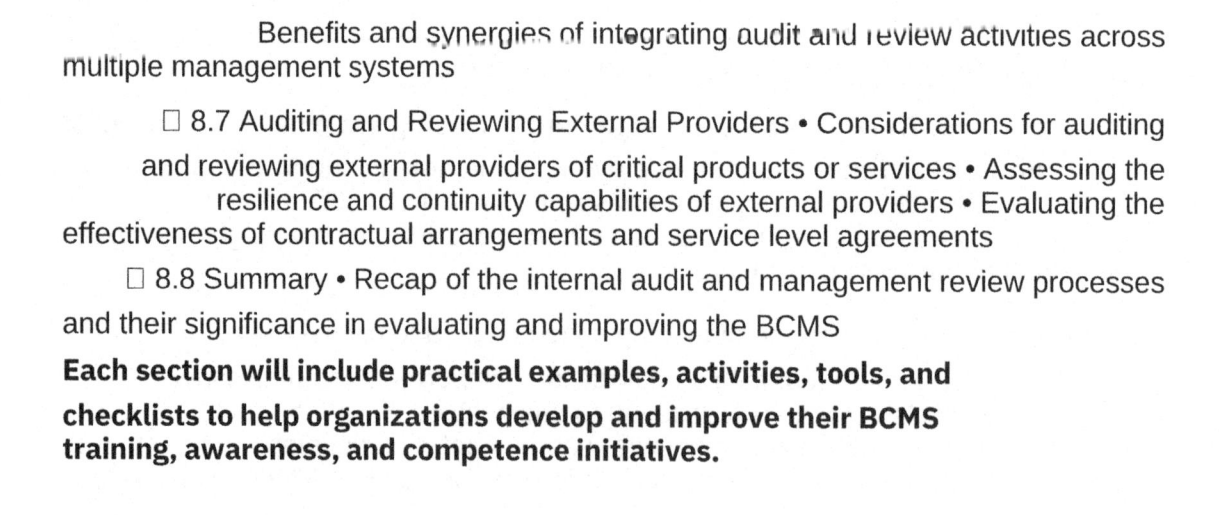

Each section will include practical examples, activities, tools, and checklists to help organizations develop and improve their BCMS training, awareness, and competence initiatives.

CHAPTER 8

Internal Audit and Management Review

8.1 Introduction

□The significance of internal audit and management review in ISO 22301 compliance

hapter 8: Internal Audit and Management Review 8.1 Introduction • The compliance and the effective functioning of a Business Continuity Management System (BCMS). These processes play a vital role in evaluating the performance, identifying areas for improvement, and ensuring the ongoing effectiveness of the BCMS.

Internal audit involves the systematic and independent examination of the BCMS to determine whether it conforms to the requirements of ISO 22301 and the organization's established policies and procedures. It helps identify gaps, non-conformities, and opportunities for improvement. Internal audits are conducted by qualified personnel who are independent of the audited activities.

Management review, on the other hand, involves a periodic evaluation of the BCMS by top management. It provides a comprehensive overview of the BCMS's performance, effectiveness, and alignment with strategic objectives. Management review ensures that the BCMS remains relevant, efficient, and capable of addressing the organization's business continuity needs.

By conducting internal audits and management reviews, organizations can:

1. **Evaluate Compliance**: Internal audits help assess the organization's compliance with ISO 22301 requirements, regulatory obligations, and internal policies. They identify areas where the BCMS may fall short and prompt corrective actions to address any non-conformities.

2. **Identify Areas for Improvement**: Internal audits and management reviews help identify areas for improvement in the BCMS. By examining processes, procedures, and performance data, organizations can pinpoint weaknesses, inefficiencies, or gaps in their business continuity practices. These findings provide valuable insights for implementing corrective actions and driving continual improvement.

3. **Ensure Ongoing Effectiveness**: Internal audits and management reviews ensure the ongoing effectiveness of the BCMS. They validate that the BCMS remains aligned with organizational objectives, adapts to changes in the business environment, and addresses emerging risks. Regular assessments

allow organizations to stay proactive and responsive in managing business continuity risks.

4. **Drive Continual Improvement**: Internal audit findings and management review outcomes inform the organization's continual improvement initiatives. By analyzing the results, organizations can identify improvement opportunities, set objectives, implement corrective actions, and monitor progress. This iterative process enables organizations to enhance the performance and resilience of their BCMS over time.

5. **Demonstrate Commitment**: Internal audits and management reviews demonstrate the organization's commitment to maintaining a robust BCMS. They provide evidence of top management's involvement and oversight, as well as the organization's dedication to meeting ISO 22301 requirements and achieving business continuity objectives. This commitment enhances stakeholder confidence and trust.

6. **Integrate with Other Management Systems**: Internal audit and management review processes can be integrated with other ISO management system standards, such as quality management (ISO 9001) or information security management (ISO 27001). Integration promotes synergies, streamlines audit and review activities, and facilitates the alignment of business processes across multiple management systems.

In summary, internal audit and management review are essential for ensuring ISO 22301 compliance and maintaining the effectiveness of the BCMS. These processes enable organizations to evaluate their performance, identify improvement opportunities, and drive continual enhancement of their business continuity capabilities. By embracing internal audits and management reviews, organizations can strengthen their resilience and adaptability in the face of potential disruptions.

8.2 The Role of Internal Audit in BCMS

Understanding the concept and purpose of an internal audit

Internal audit is a systematic and independent examination process that assesses the adequacy, effectiveness, and compliance of an organization's systems, processes, and controls. It is conducted by qualified personnel who are independent of the audited activities. The purpose of an internal audit is to provide assurance and guidance to management and stakeholders on the organization's risk management, internal controls, and governance processes.

The concept of an internal audit is rooted in the need for objective and unbiased evaluations of an organization's operations. Internal audits provide an independent and objective assessment of whether the organization's activities are aligned with its objectives, policies, procedures, and applicable regulatory requirements. It helps ensure that the organization's resources are utilized efficiently, risks are identified and managed appropriately, and governance processes are effective.

The primary objectives of an internal audit are:

1. **Risk Assessment**: Assess the effectiveness of the organization's risk management processes in identifying, evaluating, and mitigating risks. This includes evaluating the adequacy of controls in place to manage risks effectively.

2. **Compliance Verification**: Verify compliance with applicable laws, regulations, industry standards, and internal policies. Internal audits ensure that the organization is operating within the legal and regulatory framework and adhering to established guidelines.

3. **Operational Efficiency**: Evaluate the efficiency and effectiveness of the organization's operations and processes. Internal audits identify opportunities to improve operational efficiency, streamline processes, and reduce waste or redundancies.

4. **Control Evaluation**: Assess the adequacy and effectiveness of internal controls in safeguarding assets, ensuring data integrity, and mitigating operational, financial, and compliance risks.

5. **Governance and Ethics**: Evaluate the organization's governance framework, including the ethical standards and code of conduct. Internal audits help identify any gaps or deficiencies in the governance processes and recommend improvements.

6. **Information and Reporting**: Provide reliable and relevant information to management and stakeholders regarding the organization's risk management, internal controls, and governance processes. This includes communicating audit findings, recommendations, and corrective actions to facilitate informed decision-making.

In summary, the purpose of an internal audit is to provide an independent and objective assessment of an organization's risk management, internal controls, and governance processes. It helps management and stakeholders gain assurance that the organization is operating effectively, complying with regulations, managing risks appropriately, and continuously improving its operations. Internal audits play a vital role in driving accountability, transparency, and the overall success of the organization.

Key steps and best practices for conducting an internal BCMS audit

Conducting an internal Business Continuity Management System (BCMS) audit involves several key steps and best practices to ensure its effectiveness. Here are the key steps and best practices for conducting an internal BCMS audit:

1. **Establish the Audit Objectives**: Clearly define the objectives and scope of the audit. Determine the specific areas, processes, or activities that will be audited within the BCMS.

2. **Plan the Audit**: Develop an audit plan that outlines the audit scope, objectives, criteria, and timeline. Identify the resources, including personnel

and tools, required for the audit. Consider any relevant legal or regulatory requirements and organizational policies.

3. **Gather Audit Evidence**: Collect and review relevant documents, records, and data to assess the effectiveness of the BCMS. This may include policies, procedures, risk assessments, incident reports, recovery plans, training records, and other documentation.

4. **Conduct Interviews and Observations**: Engage with key personnel involved in the BCMS implementation to gain insights into their roles, responsibilities, and adherence to procedures. Observe the implementation of BCMS processes and practices firsthand to evaluate their effectiveness.

5. **Evaluate Compliance and Performance**: Assess the organization's compliance with ISO 22301 requirements, regulatory obligations, and internal policies. Evaluate the performance of the BCMS by comparing its actual implementation with established objectives, targets, and performance indicators.

6. **Identify Non-Conformities and Improvement Opportunities**: Identify any gaps, non-compliance, weaknesses, or areas for improvement within the BCMS. Document these findings in a clear and concise manner, along with the associated risks and potential impacts.

7. **Report Audit Findings**: Prepare an audit report that communicates the audit findings, including both positive aspects and areas needing improvement. Present the findings in a structured format, supported by evidence and recommendations for corrective actions.

8. **Follow-up and Monitoring**: Track the implementation of corrective actions and monitor their effectiveness. Ensure that identified non-conformities are addressed in a timely manner and that appropriate preventive measures are taken to mitigate future risks.

9. **Continual Improvement**: Use the audit findings to drive continual improvement within the BCMS. Share the lessons learned, best practices, and improvement opportunities with relevant stakeholders to enhance the effectiveness of the BCMS.

Best practices for conducting an internal BCMS audit include:

☐ Maintaining independence and objectivity throughout the audit process.

☐ Applying a risk-based approach to focus on critical areas and processes within the BCMS.

☐ Involving auditors with appropriate knowledge, skills, and experience in business continuity management.

☐ Engaging with key stakeholders to gather diverse perspectives and insights.

☐ Adhering to professional auditing standards, such as ISO 19011, to ensure the audit process is thorough and consistent.

☐ Keeping abreast of relevant industry trends, best practices, and regulatory requirements to ensure the audit is comprehensive and up to date.

☐ Promoting open communication and collaboration between auditors and auditees to foster a positive and constructive audit environment.

☐ Documenting audit procedures, findings, and recommendations systematically for future reference and follow-up.

By following these key steps and best practices, organizations can conduct effective internal BCMS audits that provide valuable insights, drive improvement, and enhance the resilience of their business continuity capabilities.

8.3 Audit Planning and Preparation

☐ How to develop an audit plan

Developing an audit plan is a crucial step in conducting an effective internal audit of a Business Continuity Management System (BCMS). Here are the key steps to develop an audit plan:

1. **Define Audit Objectives**: Clearly articulate the purpose and objectives of the audit. Determine what you want to achieve through the audit, such as assessing compliance with ISO 22301 requirements, evaluating the effectiveness of the BCMS, or identifying areas for improvement.

2. **Identify the Scope**: Determine the scope of the audit, which specifies the processes, activities, departments, or locations that will be audited. Consider the criticality and complexity of these areas, as well as any specific risks or requirements that need to be addressed.

3. **Establish Criteria**: Define the criteria against which the audit will be conducted. This includes ISO 22301 requirements, applicable laws and regulations, internal policies and procedures, industry best practices, and any other relevant standards or benchmarks.

4. **Select Audit Methods and Techniques**: Determine the audit methods and techniques that will be used to gather information and assess compliance and effectiveness. This may include document reviews, interviews, observations, data analysis, and sampling techniques. Choose methods that are appropriate for the audit objectives and provide reliable and sufficient evidence.

5. **Allocate Resources**: Determine the resources required to conduct the audit, including the audit team members, time, budget, and any necessary tools or technology. Assign responsibilities to audit team members based on their skills and expertise.

6. **Develop an Audit Schedule**: Create a timeline for the audit, including the start and end dates, as well as the planned activities and milestones. Consider the availability of auditors and auditees, and allow sufficient time for each audit phase, such as planning, fieldwork, reporting, and follow-up.

7. **Plan the Audit Procedures**: Develop detailed procedures for each phase of the audit, including the planning, fieldwork, and reporting activities. Define the specific steps to be followed, such as conducting interviews, reviewing documents, performing tests, and analyzing data. Ensure that the procedures are consistent with auditing standards and meet the audit objectives.

8. **Identify Key Contacts**: Identify the key personnel within the organization who will be involved in the audit, such as process owners, BCMS coordinators, or other relevant stakeholders. Establish communication channels and schedules for engaging with them during the audit process.

9. **Consider Risks and Controls**: Assess the risks associated with the audit and develop strategies to mitigate them. Consider potential conflicts of interest, confidentiality requirements, and the need to maintain objectivity throughout the audit. Identify any controls or safeguards that should be in place to ensure the integrity and reliability of the audit process.

10. **Review and Approval**: Review the audit plan with the audit team, relevant stakeholders, and management to ensure alignment with expectations and objectives. Seek approval from management or the audit committee before proceeding with the audit.

By following these steps, organizations can develop a comprehensive audit plan that sets the foundation for a successful internal audit of their BCMS. The plan helps ensure that the audit is conducted systematically, efficiently, and in line with the organization's objectives and requirements.

Preparing for the audit: gathering information, creating checklists, and scheduling the audit

Preparing for an audit is essential to ensure a smooth and effective process. Here are the key steps for preparing for an audit, including gathering information, creating checklists, and scheduling the audit:

1. **Understand the Audit Scope**: Review the audit objectives, scope, and criteria defined in the audit plan. Familiarize yourself with the specific areas, processes, or activities that will be audited within the Business Continuity Management System (BCMS).

2. **Gather Relevant Information**: Collect all relevant documentation related to the BCMS, such as policies, procedures, plans, incident records, risk assessments, and previous audit reports. Ensure that the information is organized and easily accessible for reference during the audit.

3. **Create Audit Checklists**: Develop audit checklists based on the audit criteria and objectives. These checklists will serve as a guide during the audit to ensure that all relevant areas are examined, and compliance with ISO 22301 requirements is assessed. The checklists can include specific questions, criteria to be evaluated, and space for recording observations and findings.

4. **Schedule the Audit**: Coordinate with the audit team, auditees, and relevant stakeholders to determine the most suitable dates and times for conducting

the audit. Consider the availability of key personnel and ensure sufficient time is allocated for each audit phase, including planning, fieldwork, reporting, and follow-up.

5. **Communicate with Auditees**: Notify the auditees about the upcoming audit and provide them with necessary information, such as the audit objectives, scope, and expectations. Schedule interviews and on-site visits with the relevant personnel to gather information and conduct assessments.

6. **Review Previous Audit Findings**: If there have been previous audits, review the findings and recommendations to understand any areas that required improvement or corrective actions. This will help provide context and continuity to the current audit and enable a follow-up on the implementation of previous recommendations.

7. **Prepare the Audit Team**: Brief the audit team members about the audit objectives, scope, and checklists. Ensure that the team members are familiar with the BCMS requirements, ISO 22301 standards, and the audit process. Assign specific roles and responsibilities to each team member based on their expertise and experience.

8. **Create an Audit Schedule**: Develop a detailed schedule that outlines the activities to be performed during each phase of the audit. This includes specific times for interviews, document reviews, observations, and any other audit procedures. Share the schedule with the auditees to ensure their availability and cooperation.

9. **Coordinate with Management**: Inform top management and relevant stakeholders about the upcoming audit and seek their support and cooperation. Obtain necessary permissions or access rights to perform the audit activities effectively.

10. **Ensure Confidentiality and Security**: Establish protocols to ensure the confidentiality and security of sensitive information encountered during the audit. Determine how audit records and findings will be stored and protected, and comply with any legal or organizational requirements regarding data privacy and security.

By following these steps, organizations can effectively prepare for an audit, ensuring that the necessary information is gathered, checklists are created, and the audit is scheduled in a manner that accommodates all stakeholders involved. Adequate preparation lays the groundwork for a successful and efficient audit of the BCMS.

8.4 Conducting the Internal Audit

- Step-by-step guide on conducting the internal audit

Conducting an internal audit of a Business Continuity Management System (BCMS) involves several key steps. Here is a step-by-step guide on conducting the internal audit:

1. **Plan the Audit**: Review the audit objectives, scope, and criteria outlined in the audit plan. Familiarize yourself with the BCMS documentation and relevant requirements, such as ISO 22301 standards. Develop an audit schedule that outlines the timeline and activities for each phase of the audit.

2. **Perform an Entry Meeting**: Start the audit by conducting an entry meeting with the auditee(s). Explain the purpose and scope of the audit, confirm their understanding, and address any initial questions or concerns. Discuss the audit process, expected outcomes, and the roles and responsibilities of both the auditors and auditees.

3. **Gather Evidence**: Collect evidence to assess the implementation and effectiveness of the BCMS. This can include reviewing documents, records, policies, procedures, incident reports, training materials, and other relevant information. Use audit checklists to guide your assessment and ensure all required areas are covered.

4. **Conduct Interviews**: Engage in interviews with key personnel involved in the BCMS implementation. This can include BCMS coordinators, process owners, and employees responsible for business continuity activities. Ask questions to gather information about their roles, responsibilities, awareness of procedures, and adherence to the BCMS requirements.

5. **Perform Observations**: Observe the implementation of BCMS processes and practices. This may involve observing drills or exercises, inspecting physical infrastructure, or witnessing emergency response procedures. Document your observations and compare them against the documented procedures and standards.

6. **Analyze and Evaluate Findings**: Analyze the collected evidence, interviews, and observations to assess the BCMS's compliance, effectiveness, and performance. Compare the findings against the audit criteria and ISO 22301 requirements. Identify any non-conformities, deficiencies, areas for improvement, or best practices.

7. **Prepare Audit Findings**: Document the audit findings in a clear and structured manner. Include a description of the non-conformities or areas of concern, along with supporting evidence and references to the relevant BCMS documentation. Ensure that the findings are objective, concise, and based on factual evidence.

8. **Discuss Findings in an Exit Meeting**: Schedule an exit meeting with the auditee(s) to discuss the audit findings. Present the audit findings, including any non-conformities or areas for improvement, and seek clarifications or additional information if needed. Address any questions or concerns raised by the auditee(s) and provide an opportunity for them to provide their input.

9. **Develop an Audit Report**: Prepare a comprehensive audit report that summarizes the audit objectives, scope, methodology, findings, and recommendations. Include an executive summary, details of the audit findings, and any supporting evidence. Clearly communicate the non-

conformities or areas for improvement and provide recommendations for corrective actions.

10. **Follow-up and Closeout**: Monitor the implementation of corrective actions and follow-up with the auditee(s) to ensure that the identified issues are addressed effectively. If necessary, schedule a closing meeting to discuss the status of corrective actions and confirm the closure of any non-conformities. Ensure that all audit documentation is properly stored and archived.

Throughout the audit process, maintain objectivity, professionalism, and confidentiality. Foster open communication with the auditee(s) and address any concerns or challenges that arise during the audit. Remember to adhere to relevant auditing standards and organizational policies.

By following this step-by-step guide, you can conduct a thorough and effective internal audit of the BCMS, assess compliance with ISO 22301 requirements, and identify areas for improvement to enhance the organization's business continuity capabilities.

Identifying non-conformities and areas for improvement

Identifying non-conformities and areas for improvement is a crucial part of the internal audit process. It helps organizations assess their compliance with ISO 22301 requirements and identify opportunities to enhance their Business Continuity Management System (BCMS). Here are the steps to effectively identify non-conformities and areas for improvement during an internal audit:

1. **Review Documentation**: Start by thoroughly reviewing the BCMS documentation, including policies, procedures, plans, and records. Compare the documented requirements with the actual implementation and practices observed during the audit.

2. **Use Audit Criteria**: Refer to the audit criteria established in the audit plan, which may include ISO 22301 requirements, regulatory obligations, internal policies, and industry best practices. Use these criteria as a reference to evaluate the BCMS's performance and identify any deviations or non-compliance.

3. **Collect Evidence**: Gather evidence through document reviews, interviews, observations, and data analysis. This evidence should support your assessment of the BCMS's compliance and effectiveness. Document your findings objectively and ensure they are based on factual evidence.

4. **Compare Practices to Requirements**: Compare the observed practices with the established requirements. Identify any gaps, deviations, or non-compliance. Look for instances where procedures are not followed, critical controls are missing, or necessary documentation is incomplete or outdated.

5. **Assess Performance**: Evaluate the effectiveness of the BCMS in meeting its objectives. Consider factors such as the frequency and quality of risk assessments, incident response capabilities, training and awareness programs, and the organization's ability to recover from disruptions.

6. **Identify Non-Conformities**: Identify specific instances where the BCMS fails to meet the established requirements. These are considered non-conformities. Non-conformities can range from minor deviations to significant breaches of compliance. Document each non-conformity with a clear description, evidence, and references to the relevant requirements.

7. **Analyze Root Causes**: Explore the root causes of the identified non-conformities. Determine why the deviations occurred and whether there are underlying systemic issues, such as inadequate training, lack of resources, or flawed processes. Understanding the root causes helps in developing effective corrective actions.

8. **Identify Areas for Improvement**: Apart from non-conformities, identify areas where the BCMS can be improved, even if they do not directly violate requirements. Look for opportunities to enhance efficiency, effectiveness, and the overall resilience of the BCMS. These areas can be related to risk management, incident response, communication strategies, or training programs.

9. **Document Findings**: Clearly document all non-conformities and areas for improvement. Include a description of the issues, supporting evidence, and references to the applicable requirements or best practices. Use a consistent format to ensure clarity and facilitate follow-up actions.

10. **Provide Recommendations**: Propose recommendations for addressing the identified non-conformities and areas for improvement. These recommendations should be practical, feasible, and tailored to the organization's context. Focus on actions that can enhance the BCMS's compliance, effectiveness, and ability to mitigate business continuity risks.

By following these steps, organizations can effectively identify non-conformities and areas for improvement during the internal audit process. This provides valuable insights for enhancing the BCMS, strengthening compliance with ISO 22301, and improving the organization's overall business continuity capabilities.

8.5 Post-Audit Activities

How to compile an audit report

Compiling an audit report is a critical step in the internal audit process. The audit report provides a comprehensive summary of the audit findings, including non-conformities, areas for improvement, and recommendations. Here are the key steps to effectively compile an audit report:

1. **Introduction**: Begin the report with an introduction that provides an overview of the audit, including the purpose, scope, and timeframe. Briefly describe the audited processes, departments, or areas within the Business Continuity Management System (BCMS).

2. **Audit Objectives**: Clearly state the objectives of the audit, which may include assessing compliance with ISO 22301 requirements, evaluating the

effectiveness of the BCMS, or identifying areas for improvement. Align the objectives with the audit plan and communicate their significance.

3. **Audit Methodology**: Describe the audit methodology employed, including the techniques used, such as document reviews, interviews, observations, and data analysis. Explain how the evidence was collected and evaluated to support the audit findings.

4. **Audit Findings**: Present the audit findings in a clear and structured manner. Start with a summary of the overall findings, highlighting any major non-conformities or critical areas for improvement. Then, provide detailed information on each non-conformity or area for improvement, including a description of the issue, supporting evidence, and references to the applicable requirements.

5. **Root Cause Analysis**: Conduct a root cause analysis for each identified non-conformity or area for improvement. Explore the underlying causes of the issues and identify any systemic or recurring problems. This analysis helps in understanding the reasons behind the non-conformities and facilitates the development of effective corrective actions.

6. **Recommendations**: Provide practical and actionable recommendations for addressing the identified non-conformities and areas for improvement. Ensure that the recommendations are aligned with the organization's objectives, resources, and capabilities. Clearly articulate the expected benefits and potential impacts of implementing the recommendations.

7. **Management Response**: Include a section for management's response to the audit findings and recommendations. This allows management to acknowledge the findings, express their commitment to addressing the issues, and outline their proposed actions or corrective measures. Encourage management to provide a timeline for implementation and assign responsibility to appropriate personnel.

8. **Conclusion**: Summarize the main findings, recommendations, and management's response in the conclusion section. Emphasize the importance of addressing the identified issues for improving the BCMS's compliance, effectiveness, and overall business continuity capabilities.

9. **Appendices**: Attach any supporting documentation, such as audit checklists, interview transcripts, or additional evidence that may be relevant to the audit findings. Include these appendices as separate sections at the end of the report.

10. **Review and Distribution**: Review the audit report thoroughly for accuracy, clarity, and consistency. Ensure that it is free from grammatical errors and typos. Obtain the necessary approvals and distribute the report to relevant stakeholders, such as top management, auditees, and other individuals responsible for implementing corrective actions.

Remember to maintain professionalism, objectivity, and confidentiality throughout the audit report compilation process. Present the findings in an impartial and evidence-based manner, focusing on providing valuable insights and recommendations to enhance the BCMS.

By following these steps, organizations can compile an audit report that effectively communicates the audit findings, non-conformities, areas for improvement, and recommendations. This facilitates the organization's understanding of the BCMS's strengths and weaknesses and supports the implementation of corrective actions to improve its overall resilience.

Communicating audit results to stakeholders

Communicating audit results to stakeholders is a crucial step in the internal audit process. It ensures that the findings, recommendations, and implications are effectively conveyed to the relevant individuals and groups. Here are the key considerations when communicating audit results to stakeholders:

1. **Identify the Stakeholders**: Determine the key stakeholders who should receive the audit results. This may include top management, department heads, BCMS coordinators, auditees, and other individuals responsible for implementing corrective actions. Consider the level of their involvement in the BCMS and their roles in driving improvements.

2. **Tailor the Message**: Adapt the communication style and content to suit the specific needs of each stakeholder. Tailor the message based on their level of technical knowledge, their roles and responsibilities, and their interest in the BCMS. Use language that is clear, concise, and free from jargon to ensure the information is easily understood.

3. **Organize the Information**: Structure the audit results in a logical and coherent manner. Present the findings, non-conformities, areas for improvement, and recommendations in a way that is easy to follow. Consider using headings, bullet points, tables, or graphs to enhance clarity and readability.

4. **Highlight Key Findings**: Emphasize the most significant audit findings and their potential impacts on the BCMS and the organization. Clearly communicate any non-conformities or critical areas for improvement that require immediate attention. Focus on providing a balanced view of both strengths and weaknesses identified during the audit.

5. **Provide Context**: Explain the context and significance of the audit findings. Help stakeholders understand how the findings relate to the organization's business continuity objectives, regulatory requirements, and industry best practices. Provide relevant background information to ensure a comprehensive understanding of the audit results.

6. **Clarify Recommendations**: Clearly articulate the recommendations derived from the audit findings. Explain why the recommendations are necessary and how they can contribute to enhancing the BCMS's compliance, effectiveness, and resilience. Provide practical guidance and encourage stakeholders to seek clarification if needed.

7. **Encourage Dialogue**: Foster an open and collaborative environment for stakeholders to ask questions, seek clarification, and provide their input on the audit results. Encourage discussions around the implications of the findings and recommendations and how they can be implemented effectively. Address any concerns or misconceptions promptly.

8. **Discuss Action Plans**: Engage stakeholders in developing action plans to address the identified non-conformities and areas for improvement. Facilitate the creation of realistic timelines, assign responsibilities, and define measurable goals for implementing corrective actions. Seek their commitment and involvement in driving the necessary improvements.

9. **Follow-Up Communication**: Establish mechanisms for ongoing communication and reporting on the progress of corrective actions. Regularly update stakeholders on the status of the implementation, milestones achieved, and any challenges encountered. Maintain transparency and provide opportunities for stakeholders to share their feedback.

10. **Document and Archive**: Keep a record of the communication of the audit results, including the distribution list, dates, and any relevant correspondence. Archive the audit report and related documentation for future reference and as evidence of the organization's commitment to continuous improvement.

Effective communication of audit results to stakeholders fosters understanding, engagement, and commitment to addressing the identified issues and driving improvements in the BCMS. By considering the specific needs of each stakeholder and delivering the information in a clear and meaningful way, organizations can maximize the impact of the audit results and promote a culture of accountability and resilience.

Developing an action plan to address identified issues

Developing an action plan is crucial to address the identified issues and implement corrective actions resulting from the internal audit. An action plan provides a structured approach to improve the Business Continuity Management System (BCMS) and enhance the organization's resilience. Here are the key steps to develop an action plan:

1. **Review Audit Findings**: Thoroughly review the audit findings, including non-conformities, areas for improvement, and recommendations. Understand the nature, severity, and implications of each issue. Prioritize the findings based on their impact on the BCMS and the organization's business continuity objectives.

2. **Assign Responsibilities**: Assign clear responsibilities to individuals or teams for addressing each finding or recommendation. Identify the key personnel who will be accountable for implementing the corrective actions. Ensure that the assigned individuals have the necessary authority, resources, and expertise to drive the improvements.

3. **Set Objectives and Goals**: Establish specific objectives and measurable goals for each corrective action. Define what needs to be achieved, by when,

and how success will be measured. Use the SMART (Specific, Measurable, Achievable, Relevant, Time-bound) framework to ensure that the objectives are well-defined and attainable.

4. **Develop Action Steps**: Break down each corrective action into actionable steps. Define the tasks, activities, and milestones required to achieve the objectives. Determine the sequence and dependencies of the steps to ensure a logical flow. Allocate sufficient time and resources for each action step.

5. **Establish Timelines**: Set realistic timelines for the implementation of each corrective action. Consider the complexity of the actions, available resources, and organizational priorities. Ensure that the timelines are achievable and aligned with the overall business continuity objectives. Create a timeline or Gantt chart to visualize the schedule and track progress.

6. **Allocate Resources**: Identify the necessary resources, such as financial, human, technological, and physical resources, needed to implement the corrective actions. Allocate resources appropriately to support the action plan. Ensure that the assigned resources are aware of their roles and responsibilities in executing the actions.

7. **Develop Monitoring and Reporting Mechanisms**: Establish mechanisms to monitor and track the progress of the action plan. Define key performance indicators (KPIs) or metrics to measure the effectiveness of the corrective actions. Implement regular reporting to keep stakeholders informed about the progress, challenges, and achievements.

8. **Implement Risk Management Measures**: Evaluate the potential risks and barriers to implementing the corrective actions. Develop risk management measures to mitigate or address these risks effectively. Monitor and update the risk management measures throughout the implementation of the action plan.

9. **Communicate and Engage**: Communicate the action plan and its objectives to all relevant stakeholders, including top management, employees, and other key individuals involved in the BCMS. Ensure their understanding, commitment, and support. Encourage feedback, suggestions, and collaboration to enhance the effectiveness of the action plan.

10. **Monitor, Evaluate, and Adjust**: Continuously monitor the progress of the action plan and evaluate the effectiveness of the implemented corrective actions. Measure the achieved outcomes against the defined objectives and KPIs. Make adjustments and refinements as needed to ensure continuous improvement.

By following these steps, organizations can develop a comprehensive action plan to address the identified issues from the internal audit and drive improvements in the BCMS. The action plan provides a roadmap for implementing the necessary changes, enhancing compliance with ISO 22301 requirements, and strengthening the organization's business continuity capabilities.

8.6 Management Review of the BCMS

Understanding the purpose and process of a management review

A management review is a critical component of the Business Continuity Management System (BCMS) and ISO 22301 compliance. It provides a structured and systematic approach for top management to assess the performance, effectiveness, and continual improvement of the BCMS. Here's an overview of the purpose and process of a management review:

Purpose of a Management Review:

1. **Assess BCMS Performance**: Evaluate the performance of the BCMS in meeting its objectives, complying with ISO 22301 requirements, and addressing business continuity risks and opportunities.

2. **Monitor Compliance**: Review the organization's compliance with applicable laws, regulations, and contractual obligations related to business continuity.

3. **Identify Improvement Opportunities**: Identify areas for improvement in the BCMS, including processes, procedures, resources, and capabilities, to enhance the organization's resilience.

4. **Review Effectiveness of Corrective Actions**: Evaluate the effectiveness of previously implemented corrective actions to address non-conformities and areas for improvement identified in audits or incidents.

5. **Review Key Performance Indicators (KPIs)**: Assess the performance of BCMS-related KPIs and metrics to gauge the effectiveness of the BCMS in achieving its objectives.

6. **Engage Stakeholders**: Provide a platform for top management to engage with stakeholders, including BCMS coordinators, process owners, and other relevant personnel, to obtain their input and feedback.

Process of a Management Review:

1. **Preparation**: Gather relevant information and data to support the management review, such as internal audit reports, incident reports, KPIs, performance data, and any changes to the BCMS since the last review. Ensure that the necessary documentation is available for review.

2. **Schedule the Review**: Set a date and time for the management review, ensuring that key stakeholders, including top management, can attend. Provide advance notice and share the agenda to allow participants to prepare.

3. **Conduct the Review Meeting**: Facilitate the management review meeting, typically led by the top management representative or the BCMS coordinator. The meeting should cover the following aspects:

    ☐ Review of the BCMS policy, objectives, and alignment with the organization's strategic direction.

☐ Discussion and analysis of audit findings, non-conformities, and areas for improvement.

☐ Examination of incident reports and the effectiveness of incident response and recovery activities.

☐ Evaluation of KPIs, performance metrics, and targets.

☐ Review of the effectiveness of implemented corrective actions.

☐ Assessment of resource allocation, including human, financial, and technological resources.

☐ Consideration of external factors and changes that may impact the BCMS.

☐ Engagement with stakeholders to gather their input and feedback.

4. **Document the Review**: Record the key discussions, decisions, and outcomes of the management review meeting. Document the identified improvement opportunities, decisions made, and any required actions or follow-up activities.

5. **Implement Actions and Follow-up**: Assign responsibilities for implementing the actions and improvements identified during the management review. Set timelines, allocate resources, and track progress. Ensure appropriate follow-up measures are in place to monitor the implementation and effectiveness of the actions.

6. **Review the Effectiveness of Actions**: Conduct subsequent management reviews to evaluate the progress made in implementing the actions and improvements. Assess the effectiveness of the actions in addressing non-conformities and areas for improvement. Make adjustments and refinements as necessary.

7. **Maintain Records**: Keep records of management review meetings, including agendas, minutes, action plans, and outcomes. Archive these records for future reference and as evidence of the organization's commitment to continual improvement.

The management review provides an opportunity for top management to demonstrate their commitment to the BCMS, drive improvements, and ensure the ongoing effectiveness of the system. It enables strategic

☐**Key inputs and outputs of a management review**

During a management review, several inputs and outputs contribute to the process. These inputs provide information and data for review, while the outputs capture the outcomes and decisions made during the review. Here are the key inputs and outputs of a management review:

Inputs:

1. **BCMS Documentation**: The BCMS documentation, including policies, procedures, plans, and records, serves as a fundamental input for the management review. It provides a basis for assessing the BCMS's performance, compliance, and effectiveness.

2. **Internal Audit Reports**: Internal audit reports highlight the findings, non-conformities, and areas for improvement identified during the audit process. They provide valuable insights into the BCMS's performance and help prioritize the areas to be reviewed.

3. **Incident Reports**: Incident reports document any business disruptions, incidents, or near-miss events that have occurred since the last management review. They provide information on the effectiveness of the BCMS in responding to and recovering from incidents.

4. **Key Performance Indicators (KPIs)**: KPIs and performance metrics relevant to the BCMS offer quantitative data on the system's performance and effectiveness. They provide insights into areas such as risk mitigation, recovery objectives, training effectiveness, and incident response times.

5. **Feedback from Stakeholders**: Input from stakeholders, including employees, BCMS coordinators, process owners, and other relevant individuals, is valuable in understanding the practical application of the BCMS and gathering perspectives on its performance and areas for improvement.

Outputs:

1. **Management Review Report**: The management review report summarizes the outcomes of the review, including discussions, decisions, and identified improvement opportunities. It provides a record of the management review process, outcomes, and actions to be taken.

2. **Action Plans**: Action plans capture the decisions made during the management review regarding the implementation of corrective actions and improvement initiatives. They outline the specific actions, responsibilities, timelines, and resources required to address the identified issues.

3. **Revised BCMS Documentation**: If necessary, the management review may result in updates or revisions to the BCMS documentation. This can include changes to policies, procedures, plans, or other documents to reflect the decisions and improvements identified during the review.

4. **Updated KPIs and Metrics**: Based on the outcomes of the management review, the KPIs and metrics used to measure BCMS performance may be revised or refined. This ensures that the metrics align with the organization's objectives and accurately reflect the effectiveness of the BCMS.

5. **Communication and Follow-up**: The management review outcomes are communicated to relevant stakeholders, including top management, employees, and other individuals responsible for implementing the identified

actions. This ensures transparency, shared understanding, and commitment to driving improvements.

These inputs and outputs play a crucial role in the management review process, providing the necessary information and driving the actions needed to continually improve the BCMS. They contribute to the organization's ability to assess the effectiveness of the BCMS, comply with ISO 22301 requirements, and enhance its business continuity capabilities.

8.7 Conducting the Management Review

▢ How to prepare for the management review

Preparing for a management review is essential to ensure a smooth and effective process. Here are the key steps to prepare for a management review:

1. **Establish Objectives**: Clearly define the objectives of the management review. Determine what you aim to achieve through the review process, such as assessing BCMS performance, identifying improvement opportunities, or monitoring compliance with ISO 22301 requirements. Align the objectives with the organization's business continuity goals.

2. **Gather Relevant Information**: Collect all the necessary information and data required for the management review. This includes internal audit reports, incident reports, performance metrics, KPIs, BCMS documentation, and any changes or updates to the system since the last review. Ensure that the information is accurate, up-to-date, and easily accessible.

3. **Review Previous Management Review Outcomes**: Study the outcomes and action plans from previous management reviews. Assess the progress made in implementing previous decisions and actions. Identify any outstanding items or recurring issues that need to be addressed in the current review.

4. **Prepare an Agenda**: Develop a detailed agenda for the management review meeting. Outline the topics to be discussed, the order of presentation, and the estimated time for each agenda item. Share the agenda with the participants in advance to allow them to prepare and contribute effectively during the review.

5. **Identify Stakeholders**: Determine the key stakeholders who should participate in the management review. This typically includes top management, BCMS coordinators, relevant department heads, and individuals responsible for key BCMS processes. Ensure their availability and involvement in the review process.

6. **Assign Roles and Responsibilities**: Designate a facilitator or a management representative responsible for coordinating the management review process. Clarify the roles and responsibilities of each participant, such as presenting specific topics, providing relevant data, or leading discussions on certain areas.

7. **Conduct a Pre-Review Meeting**: Hold a pre-review meeting with the key participants to discuss the purpose, objectives, and expectations of the management review. Share the agenda, review the documentation, and address any questions or concerns. Ensure everyone understands their roles and responsibilities during the review.

8. **Prepare Presentation Materials**: Prepare visual aids, such as slides or documents, to support the presentations during the management review. Summarize the key findings, non-conformities, areas for improvement, and recommendations in a concise and clear manner. Use visuals, charts, or graphs to enhance understanding.

9. **Ensure Adequate Time and Resources**: Allocate sufficient time for the management review process, considering the complexity of the BCMS, the number of participants, and the depth of discussions. Ensure that the necessary resources, such as meeting rooms, audiovisual equipment, and relevant documentation, are readily available.

10. **Promote Engagement and Participation**: Encourage active participation and engagement from all stakeholders during the management review. Foster an open and collaborative environment that allows for constructive discussions, sharing of insights, and diverse perspectives. Create opportunities for stakeholders to provide their input and feedback.

By following these steps, you can effectively prepare for a management review, ensuring that the process is well-organized, productive, and aligned with the organization's objectives. Proper preparation sets the foundation for a successful management review and facilitates the identification of improvement opportunities and actions to enhance the BCMS.

Guidelines for conducting an effective review

Conducting an effective management review is crucial to ensure that the review process yields valuable insights, decisions, and actions for improving the Business Continuity Management System (BCMS). Here are some guidelines to help you conduct an effective review:

1. **Define Clear Objectives**: Clearly define the objectives and scope of the management review. Align the objectives with the organization's business continuity goals, ISO 22301 compliance requirements, and the purpose of the review. This provides a clear focus and direction for the review process.

2. **Engage Relevant Stakeholders**: Involve key stakeholders who have a direct or indirect influence on the BCMS. This typically includes top management, BCMS coordinators, process owners, and other individuals responsible for critical BCMS activities. Ensure their active participation and encourage diverse perspectives.

3. **Follow a Structured Agenda**: Develop a structured agenda that covers all the key aspects of the BCMS, such as policy compliance, risk assessment, incident management, training, and corrective actions. Allocate sufficient time

for each agenda item, allowing for comprehensive discussions and decision-making.

4. **Review Documentation and Data**: Thoroughly review relevant BCMS documentation, such as policies, procedures, plans, audit reports, incident reports, and performance data. Analyze the data and identify trends, patterns, and areas of concern. Ensure that the information is accurate, up-to-date, and readily available for review.

5. **Encourage Open and Transparent Communication**: Foster an environment of open and transparent communication during the review. Encourage participants to express their viewpoints, concerns, and suggestions freely. Create a safe space for constructive discussions and active engagement. Listen actively and address any conflicts or differing opinions.

6. **Evaluate Compliance and Performance**: Assess the compliance of the BCMS with ISO 22301 requirements and applicable laws, regulations, and contractual obligations. Evaluate the performance of the BCMS in meeting its objectives, managing risks, and achieving desired outcomes. Use performance indicators and metrics to measure progress and identify gaps.

7. **Identify Improvement Opportunities**: Identify areas for improvement in the BCMS based on the review findings. Prioritize the improvement opportunities based on their potential impact on the organization's resilience and strategic objectives. Seek input from stakeholders to gather diverse perspectives and insights.

8. **Make Decisions and Set Priorities**: Make informed decisions based on the review findings and stakeholder input. Set priorities for addressing the identified improvement opportunities and non-conformities. Allocate resources, define responsibilities, and establish realistic timelines for implementing the necessary corrective actions.

9. **Document Review Outcomes**: Document the outcomes of the management review, including decisions, action plans, and responsibilities. Clearly capture the agreed-upon improvements, corrective actions, and targets. Ensure that the documentation is accurate, complete, and accessible to relevant stakeholders for future reference.

10. **Follow-Up and Monitor Progress**: Regularly monitor the progress of the agreed-upon actions and improvement initiatives. Establish mechanisms for tracking the implementation of corrective actions, measuring the effectiveness of changes, and assessing the impact on the BCMS. Conduct periodic follow-up reviews to evaluate progress and make further refinements.

By following these guidelines, you can conduct an effective management review that drives improvements in the BCMS, promotes compliance with ISO 22301, and enhances the organization's resilience. The review process should facilitate open communication, data-driven decision-making, and the identification of actionable insights for continual improvement.

- **Follow-up activities after the management review**

After the management review, it is important to follow up on the outcomes, decisions, and actions identified during the review. This ensures that the improvements and changes discussed during the review are effectively implemented. Here are some key follow-up activities to consider:

1. **Communicate Review Outcomes**: Share the outcomes of the management review with relevant stakeholders, including top management, BCMS coordinators, and other individuals responsible for implementing the identified actions. Provide a summary of the review findings, decisions made, and agreed-upon improvement initiatives. Ensure that everyone is aware of their roles and responsibilities in driving the necessary changes.

2. **Implement Corrective Actions**: Begin implementing the corrective actions and improvement initiatives that were identified during the management review. Assign responsibilities, set timelines, and allocate resources accordingly. Establish a clear plan for implementing the changes and monitor progress to ensure that actions are completed effectively and on time.

3. **Update Documentation**: Review and update the BCMS documentation, including policies, procedures, plans, and records, as necessary. Incorporate any changes or improvements discussed during the management review. Ensure that the documentation accurately reflects the decisions made and the actions being taken.

4. **Monitor Progress**: Regularly monitor the progress of the implemented actions and improvements. Track the status of each action, ensuring that milestones and timelines are being met. Establish mechanisms for reporting progress and addressing any challenges or roadblocks encountered during implementation. Provide support and resources as needed to ensure successful execution.

5. **Evaluate Effectiveness**: Evaluate the effectiveness of the implemented actions and improvements. Assess whether the changes have achieved the desired outcomes and have had the intended impact on the BCMS. Use performance indicators and metrics to measure progress and gauge the effectiveness of the changes made.

6. **Conduct Follow-Up Reviews**: Consider conducting follow-up reviews to assess the progress made in implementing the corrective actions and improvements. Evaluate whether the identified issues have been adequately addressed and if further adjustments are required. These reviews provide an opportunity to refine the actions and make additional improvements based on the feedback received.

7. **Promote Continuous Improvement**: Foster a culture of continuous improvement within the organization. Encourage stakeholders to provide feedback, suggestions, and lessons learned from the implementation of the actions. Use this feedback to refine processes, enhance the BCMS, and drive ongoing improvement. Continually seek opportunities to enhance the organization's resilience and business continuity capabilities.

8. **Document and Share Lessons Learned**: Capture lessons learned from the management review process and the implementation of corrective actions. Document best practices, challenges encountered, and insights gained. Share these lessons learned with relevant stakeholders to promote knowledge sharing and facilitate future improvements.

By conducting thorough follow-up activities, organizations can ensure that the outcomes of the management review are effectively translated into tangible actions and improvements within the BCMS. This facilitates continual improvement, strengthens the organization's resilience, and enhances its ability to respond to and recover from disruptions.

8.8 Continuous Improvement through Audit and Review

How audits and management reviews contribute to continual improvement

Audits and management reviews play a crucial role in driving continual improvement within the Business Continuity Management System (BCMS) and the organization as a whole. Here's how audits and management reviews contribute to continual improvement:

1. **Identifying Non-Conformities and Areas for Improvement**: Audits help identify non-conformities, deviations, and gaps in the BCMS's implementation and compliance with ISO 22301 requirements. Management reviews provide a broader assessment of the BCMS's performance, effectiveness, and alignment with business objectives. By identifying these areas for improvement, audits and management reviews serve as a starting point for driving continual improvement efforts.

2. **Setting Improvement Objectives**: Through the findings of audits and discussions in management reviews, specific improvement objectives can be identified. These objectives may include enhancing process efficiency, addressing identified non-conformities, strengthening risk management practices, or improving incident response capabilities. These objectives provide a roadmap for continual improvement initiatives.

3. **Monitoring Progress and Performance**: Audits and management reviews help monitor the progress of improvement initiatives and assess the overall performance of the BCMS. Regular audits provide a mechanism to measure compliance and identify any regression or recurrence of non-conformities. Management reviews evaluate the effectiveness of improvement actions and gauge the organization's progress towards its goals. This monitoring ensures that improvement efforts stay on track and deviations are promptly addressed.

4. **Validating Corrective Actions**: Audits and management reviews verify the effectiveness of corrective actions taken to address identified non-conformities or improvement opportunities. Audits assess whether the actions have effectively resolved the identified issues, and management reviews evaluate the impact and sustainability of the implemented changes. This validation

process ensures that corrective actions have been successful and contribute to ongoing improvement.

5. **Evaluating the Effectiveness of the BCMS**: Audits and management reviews provide a mechanism to evaluate the effectiveness of the BCMS itself. They assess the system's ability to meet its objectives, manage risks, and address emerging challenges. By reviewing performance data, incident reports, and audit findings, organizations can identify areas where the BCMS may need adjustments or enhancements to ensure its ongoing effectiveness.

6. **Promoting a Culture of Learning and Adaptation**: Audits and management reviews create opportunities for learning and reflection within the organization. Through the sharing of audit findings, management review outcomes, and lessons learned, organizations can foster a culture of continuous learning, adaptation, and improvement. This culture encourages individuals and teams to seek innovative solutions, share best practices, and proactively contribute to the enhancement of the BCMS.

7. **Driving Innovation and Best Practices**: Audits and management reviews provide insights into emerging trends, industry best practices, and new technologies or methodologies relevant to business continuity. By keeping abreast of these developments, organizations can incorporate innovative approaches and best practices into their BCMS. This drives continual improvement by ensuring the BCMS remains up-to-date, effective, and aligned with industry standards.

8. **Facilitating Stakeholder Engagement**: Audits and management reviews involve engaging stakeholders at various levels. This engagement fosters a sense of ownership and collaboration, as stakeholders provide valuable input, feedback, and suggestions for improvement. By actively involving stakeholders in the review process, organizations can tap into their expertise and diverse perspectives, thereby enriching the continual improvement efforts.

By leveraging the insights gained from audits and management reviews, organizations can identify improvement opportunities, validate corrective actions, evaluate the effectiveness of the BCMS, promote a culture of learning and adaptation, and drive ongoing innovation. This continual improvement mindset ensures that the organization's business continuity capabilities remain robust, resilient, and aligned with changing business needs and industry requirements.

Strategies for leveraging audit and review findings for BCMS improvement

Leveraging audit and review findings effectively is crucial for driving improvement within the Business Continuity Management System (BCMS). Here are some strategies to make the most of audit and review findings for BCMS improvement:

1. **Analyze Findings and Identify Trends**: Thoroughly analyze the findings from audits and management reviews to identify recurring themes, trends, and common issues. Look for patterns or systemic problems that may require broader improvements rather than addressing isolated incidents. This analysis

provides insights into the root causes of non-conformities or performance gaps, enabling targeted improvement efforts.

2. **Prioritize Improvement Opportunities**: Prioritize improvement opportunities based on their potential impact on the BCMS and the organization's objectives. Assess the severity, frequency, and potential consequences of identified issues to determine their priority. Focus on areas that have the greatest potential to enhance the resilience of critical processes, reduce risks, and improve the overall effectiveness of the BCMS.

3. **Involve Relevant Stakeholders**: Engage relevant stakeholders, including process owners, BCMS coordinators, and individuals responsible for key BCMS activities, in the improvement process. Seek their input and involvement in identifying root causes, brainstorming solutions, and implementing improvements. Collaboration and diverse perspectives help generate innovative ideas and enhance the ownership and commitment to the improvement initiatives.

4. **Establish Clear Action Plans**: Develop clear and concise action plans that address the identified improvement opportunities. Define specific actions, responsibilities, timelines, and expected outcomes for each improvement initiative. Ensure that the action plans are realistic, measurable, and aligned with the organization's resources and priorities. Clear communication of the action plans helps drive accountability and progress.

5. **Monitor and Track Progress**: Regularly monitor the progress of improvement initiatives to ensure they are on track. Establish key performance indicators (KPIs) and metrics to measure the effectiveness of the improvements. Set milestones and review progress against the defined timelines. Regularly communicate progress to stakeholders to foster transparency and maintain momentum in the improvement efforts.

6. **Encourage Continuous Learning and Adaptation**: Create a culture of continuous learning and adaptation by encouraging feedback and sharing lessons learned from the improvement initiatives. Foster an environment where individuals and teams feel comfortable discussing challenges, suggesting improvements, and sharing best practices. Emphasize the importance of learning from failures and successes to drive ongoing improvement.

7. **Document Changes and Update Documentation**: Document the changes implemented as a result of the improvement initiatives. Update relevant BCMS documentation, including policies, procedures, plans, and records, to reflect the changes. Ensure that the updated documentation is readily accessible to relevant stakeholders. Clear and up-to-date documentation promotes consistency and facilitates understanding of the revised processes and practices.

8. **Regularly Review and Reassess**: Periodically review the effectiveness of implemented improvements and reassess the BCMS. Conduct follow-up audits or reviews to evaluate the impact of the improvements and identify any new areas for enhancement. Continually assess the evolving needs of the

organization and the changing business environment to ensure the BCMS remains aligned with strategic objectives.

9. **Promote Knowledge Sharing and Collaboration**: Encourage knowledge sharing and collaboration among different parts of the organization. Create platforms or mechanisms for sharing best practices, lessons learned, and success stories related to BCMS improvement. Facilitate cross-functional discussions and collaboration to leverage the collective knowledge and expertise within the organization.

10. **Seek External Perspectives**: Consider seeking external perspectives through benchmarking, participation in industry forums, or engaging consultants with expertise in business continuity management. External insights can provide valuable perspectives on emerging best practices, industry trends, and innovative approaches to BCMS improvement.

By employing these strategies, organizations can effectively leverage audit and review findings to drive continuous improvement in their BCMS.

8.9 Summary

Recap of the role and process of internal audit and management review in BCMS

Chapter 8 focused on the essential aspects of internal audit and management review within the Business Continuity Management System (BCMS). Let's recap the key points covered:

- Internal audits play a vital role in assessing the effectiveness of the BCMS, identifying non-conformities, and ensuring compliance with ISO 22301 requirements.

- Management reviews provide a broader evaluation of the BCMS's performance, its alignment with business objectives, and the identification of improvement opportunities.

- Internal audits and management reviews contribute to continual improvement by identifying areas for enhancement, setting improvement objectives, and monitoring progress.

- Conducting an effective internal audit involves planning, executing, and reporting on the audit findings. It includes steps such as developing an audit plan, conducting the audit, identifying non-conformities, and preparing an audit report.

- Management reviews involve evaluating the BCMS's performance, analyzing data, and making decisions based on the review outcomes. Key inputs include performance metrics, incident reports, audit findings, and stakeholder feedback, while outputs may include improvement initiatives, action plans, and changes to the BCMS.

- Effective follow-up activities after the management review include communicating review outcomes, implementing corrective actions, updating documentation, monitoring progress, conducting follow-up reviews, and promoting a culture of learning and adaptation.

- Resources, including financial, human, technological, and external resources, are critical to the successful implementation of ISO 22301 and should be appropriately allocated and managed.

- Training, awareness, and competence are essential elements for a successful BCMS. Organizations should provide training programs, raise awareness about the BCMS, and ensure that individuals possess the necessary competencies to fulfill their roles effectively.

- Internal audit and management review findings provide valuable insights for driving continual improvement within the BCMS. Organizations should analyze the findings, prioritize improvement opportunities, involve stakeholders, and establish clear action plans.

- Leveraging audit and review findings for improvement involves monitoring progress, adapting to changing circumstances, involving relevant stakeholders, updating documentation, and seeking external perspectives.

By understanding the role and process of internal audit and management review in the BCMS, organizations can effectively utilize these activities to drive continual improvement, enhance their resilience, and ensure ongoing compliance with ISO 22301 standards.

Preparing for the next stage: maintaining and improving the BCMS

- Chapter 9: Maintaining and Improving the BCMS 9.1 Introduction • The importance of maintaining and continuously improving the Business Continuity Management System (BCMS) for long-term effectiveness

- 9.2 Establishing a Culture of Continual Improvement • The role of organizational culture in promoting continual improvement • Strategies for fostering a culture of continual improvement within the organization

- 9.3 Monitoring and Measurement • The importance of monitoring and measuring BCMS performance • Key performance indicators (KPIs) for assessing the effectiveness of the BCMS • Methods for collecting and analyzing performance data

- 9.4 Internal Audits for Ongoing Compliance • The role of internal audits in maintaining BCMS compliance with ISO 22301 • Planning and conducting regular internal audits • Using audit findings to drive ongoing improvement

- 9.5 Corrective Actions and Preventive Actions • The importance of addressing non-conformities and taking corrective actions • The concept of preventive actions to proactively manage risks and prevent recurrence of issues • Developing and implementing effective corrective and preventive action plans

• 9.6 Management of Change • The significance of managing changes within the BCMS • The process for assessing and managing changes effectively • Ensuring the continuity of the BCMS during times of change

• 9.7 Incident Management and Business Continuity Exercises • The role of incident management in maintaining and improving the BCMS • The importance of conducting regular business continuity exercises • Types of exercises and their benefits

• 9.8 Continual Improvement Process • The cyclical nature of the continual improvement process • The Plan-Do-Check-Act (PDCA) cycle in the context of continual improvement • Implementing improvement initiatives and measuring their impact

• 9.9 Stakeholder Engagement and Feedback • The importance of engaging stakeholders in the continual improvement process • Methods for collecting stakeholder feedback and incorporating it into improvement efforts

• 9.10 Document Control and Version Control • The significance of proper document control in maintaining the integrity of the BCMS documentation • Establishing document control processes and version control mechanisms

• 9.11 Performance Review and Reporting • The role of performance review in assessing the effectiveness of the BCMS • Preparing and delivering regular performance reports to stakeholders • Using performance review outcomes to drive improvement

• 9.12 Summary • Recap of the key topics covered in Chapter 9

Throughout the chapter, there will be real-world examples, templates, checklists, and tips to assist organizations in conducting effective audits and management reviews, thereby fostering continual improvement.

CHAPTER 9

Maintaining and Improving the BCMS

9.1 Introduction

Understanding the importance of continuous maintenance and improvement in the BCMS

ontinuous maintenance and improvement are crucial elements of a robust and importance of continuous maintenance and improvement in the BCMS can be summarized as follows:

1. Adaptation to Changing Environments: The business landscape is dynamic, with emerging risks, technological advancements, regulatory changes, and evolving customer expectations. Continuous maintenance ensures that the BCMS remains aligned with the changing environment and enables organizations to proactively respond to potential disruptions.

2. Enhancing Resilience: Continuous improvement allows organizations to enhance their resilience by identifying and addressing gaps or weaknesses in their BCMS. By regularly reviewing and updating the BCMS, organizations can strengthen their ability to withstand and recover from disruptive events, ensuring the continuity of critical operations.

3. Meeting Compliance Requirements: Organizations are often subject to various regulatory and industry-specific requirements related to business continuity. Continuous maintenance and improvement help organizations stay compliant with these standards and regulations, reducing the risk of penalties, reputational damage, and legal implications.

4. Driving Efficiency and Effectiveness: Through regular maintenance and improvement, organizations can streamline their business continuity processes, identify areas of inefficiency, and optimize resource utilization. This, in turn, improves the overall effectiveness of the BCMS and enables organizations to achieve their business objectives more efficiently.

5. Enhancing Stakeholder Confidence: Stakeholders, including customers, partners, employees, and regulatory bodies, place trust in organizations to effectively manage potential disruptions. By demonstrating a commitment to continuous maintenance and improvement of the BCMS, organizations can enhance stakeholder confidence and build a reputation for resilience and reliability.

6. Continual Learning and Growth: Continuous improvement fosters a culture of learning within the organization. By regularly assessing the effectiveness of the

BCMS and seeking opportunities for improvement, organizations encourage ongoing learning, knowledge sharing, and skill development among employees. This promotes a proactive and resilient mindset throughout the organization.

7. Future Readiness: The business landscape is characterized by uncertainty and the potential for unforeseen events. Continuous maintenance and improvement ensure that organizations are well-prepared to respond to future disruptions effectively. By continually assessing and enhancing their BCMS, organizations can adapt to emerging risks and seize new opportunities.

In summary, continuous maintenance and improvement are essential for the long-term effectiveness and success of the BCMS. By embracing a proactive approach, organizations can enhance their resilience, meet compliance requirements, drive efficiency, build stakeholder confidence, foster a culture of learning, and stay prepared for future challenges and opportunities.

9.2 Continual Improvement in BCMS: An Overview

The concept and significance of continual improvement

Continual improvement is a fundamental concept in the Business Continuity Management System (BCMS) that emphasizes the ongoing enhancement and optimization of processes, practices, and outcomes. It involves systematically reviewing and improving the effectiveness of the BCMS to adapt to changing circumstances, address emerging risks, and achieve better results.

The significance of continual improvement in the BCMS can be summarized as follows:

1. Adapting to Changing Environments: Continual improvement allows organizations to adapt to evolving business environments, including emerging risks, technological advancements, regulatory changes, and customer expectations. It ensures that the BCMS remains relevant and effective in the face of new challenges and opportunities.

2. Identifying and Addressing Gaps: Continual improvement helps organizations identify gaps, weaknesses, and areas for enhancement within the BCMS. By regularly evaluating the system's performance and seeking feedback from stakeholders, organizations can proactively identify areas that need attention and take appropriate actions to bridge those gaps.

3. Enhancing Resilience: The primary goal of a BCMS is to enhance an organization's resilience and ensure the continuity of critical operations. Continual improvement enables organizations to strengthen their resilience by identifying vulnerabilities, improving response capabilities, and implementing preventive measures to minimize the impact of potential disruptions.

4. Driving Efficiency and Effectiveness: Continual improvement promotes the optimization of processes, procedures, and resource allocation within the BCMS. By systematically reviewing and refining the system, organizations can

streamline operations, eliminate inefficiencies, and achieve greater efficiency and effectiveness in their business continuity efforts.

5. Fostering a Culture of Learning: Continual improvement encourages a culture of learning and continuous development within the organization. It emphasizes the importance of actively seeking feedback, sharing knowledge, and embracing a mindset of continuous learning. This helps employees stay updated with best practices, industry trends, and emerging technologies, ultimately contributing to the overall success of the BCMS.

6. Stakeholder Confidence and Trust: Continual improvement demonstrates an organization's commitment to excellence and its dedication to meeting the needs and expectations of stakeholders. By actively improving the BCMS, organizations enhance stakeholder confidence, build trust, and establish a reputation for reliability and resilience.

7. Meeting Compliance Requirements: Continual improvement is closely linked to meeting regulatory and industry-specific compliance requirements. By continually assessing and enhancing the BCMS, organizations can ensure they comply with relevant standards, regulations, and legal obligations, reducing the risk of non-compliance and associated penalties.

Overall, the concept of continual improvement underscores the importance of ongoing evaluation, adjustment, and refinement of the BCMS. It enables organizations to adapt to changing circumstances, drive efficiency, enhance resilience, foster a culture of learning, and meet stakeholder expectations. By embracing continual improvement, organizations can remain agile, proactive, and better prepared to navigate the challenges and opportunities in an ever-changing business landscape.

Key strategies for fostering continual improvement in the BCMS

2 / 2

Fostering continual improvement in the Business Continuity Management System (BCMS) requires a proactive and systematic approach. Here are key strategies for fostering continual improvement in the BCMS:

1. Establish a Culture of Continuous Improvement: Create a culture within the organization that values and encourages continuous improvement. Foster an environment where employees feel empowered to identify opportunities for improvement, share ideas, and contribute to the enhancement of the BCMS.

2. Leadership Support and Engagement: Ensure that top management is actively involved and supportive of continual improvement initiatives. Leaders should demonstrate a commitment to continuous improvement, allocate resources, and provide guidance and support to drive the process.

3. Set Clear Improvement Objectives: Define specific improvement objectives for the BCMS. These objectives should align with the organization's overall strategic goals and be measurable and achievable. Clear objectives provide a focus for improvement efforts and enable progress tracking.

4. Regular Monitoring and Evaluation: Implement a systematic process for monitoring and evaluating the performance of the BCMS. Regularly assess key performance indicators (KPIs) to identify trends, measure effectiveness, and pinpoint areas for improvement.

5. Feedback and Stakeholder Engagement: Seek feedback from stakeholders, including employees, customers, partners, and regulators. Actively engage stakeholders to understand their needs, expectations, and suggestions for improvement. Incorporate their feedback into the decision-making process and improvement initiatives.

6. Continuous Training and Development: Invest in training and development programs for employees involved in the BCMS. Provide opportunities for skill-building, knowledge sharing, and staying updated with industry best practices. Continuous training enhances competencies and fosters a culture of learning and improvement.

7. Learn from Incidents and Exercises: Actively analyze and learn from real incidents, near-misses, and business continuity exercises. Identify lessons learned, root causes of failures, and areas for improvement. Use this knowledge to enhance response plans, update procedures, and strengthen the overall BCMS.

8. Establish Improvement Projects and Initiatives: Implement improvement projects to address identified gaps and opportunities for enhancement. Assign responsibilities, set timelines, and allocate resources to drive these initiatives effectively. Regularly monitor progress and make necessary adjustments as required.

9. Document and Share Best Practices: Document successful practices, lessons learned, and improvement initiatives within the BCMS. Create a repository of best practices to share knowledge across the organization and encourage the adoption of effective approaches.

10. Regular Management Review: Conduct periodic management reviews to evaluate the overall performance of the BCMS and identify improvement opportunities. Use the management review outcomes to set priorities, allocate resources, and guide future improvement initiatives.

By implementing these strategies, organizations can foster a culture of continual improvement in their BCMS. This enables them to adapt to changing circumstances, enhance resilience, drive efficiency, and maintain alignment with business objectives and stakeholder expectations. Continual improvement ensures that the BCMS remains robust, effective, and aligned with the organization's evolving needs.

9.3 Monitoring and Measuring the BCMS

Importance of regular monitoring and measurement

Regular monitoring and measurement are crucial components of maintaining and improving the effectiveness of the Business Continuity Management System (BCMS). Here are the key reasons why regular monitoring and measurement are important:

1. Performance Evaluation: Regular monitoring and measurement allow organizations to assess the performance of the BCMS against established objectives, targets, and key performance indicators (KPIs). It provides valuable insights into how well the BCMS is functioning and helps identify areas that require improvement.

2. Early Detection of Issues: Monitoring and measurement help organizations identify potential issues and weaknesses in the BCMS before they escalate into significant problems. By detecting issues early, organizations can take timely corrective actions to mitigate risks, prevent disruptions, and ensure the continuity of critical operations.

3. Compliance Monitoring: Regular monitoring and measurement ensure that the BCMS remains in compliance with relevant standards, regulations, and legal requirements. It helps organizations identify any gaps or deviations from the desired compliance levels and take necessary corrective actions to address them.

4. Performance Improvement: Monitoring and measurement provide a baseline for tracking improvements and assessing the effectiveness of improvement initiatives. By measuring performance over time, organizations can identify trends, evaluate the impact of implemented changes, and make data-driven decisions to further enhance the BCMS.

5. Decision-making and Resource Allocation: Monitoring and measurement data provide valuable information for decision-making and resource allocation. It helps organizations identify areas of priority, allocate resources effectively, and focus efforts on areas that require attention, thereby optimizing the use of resources.

6. Benchmarking and Comparison: Regular monitoring and measurement allow organizations to benchmark their BCMS performance against industry best practices and compare it with peers and competitors. This provides insights into areas where the organization excels and areas where improvements can be made, leading to a more competitive and resilient BCMS.

7. Communication and Reporting: Monitoring and measurement data serve as a basis for reporting to stakeholders, including senior management, customers, partners, and regulatory bodies. It provides evidence of the organization's commitment to the BCMS, its performance, and its ability to manage potential disruptions effectively.

8. Continuous Improvement: Monitoring and measurement play a vital role in the continual improvement process. They provide feedback on the effectiveness of implemented improvement initiatives and help organizations identify new areas for improvement. By monitoring performance, organizations can ensure that the BCMS remains dynamic, adaptive, and aligned with evolving needs and requirements.

In summary, regular monitoring and measurement are essential for evaluating the performance of the BCMS, detecting issues early, ensuring compliance, driving improvement, making informed decisions, and demonstrating the organization's commitment to effective business continuity management. It is a proactive approach to maintain a robust BCMS and enhance the organization's resilience in the face of potential disruptions.

Techniques and tools for monitoring and measuring BCMS performance

Monitoring and measuring the effectiveness of the Business Continuity Management System (BCMS) requires the use of various techniques and tools. Here are some commonly used techniques and tools for monitoring and measuring the BCMS:

1. Key Performance Indicators (KPIs): KPIs are quantifiable metrics that help assess the performance of the BCMS. They provide measurable targets against which the organization can track its progress and evaluate the effectiveness of its business continuity efforts. Examples of KPIs include recovery time objectives (RTO), recovery point objectives (RPO), testing and exercise completion rates, incident response times, and customer satisfaction ratings.

2. Audits and Assessments: Regular internal audits and assessments are essential for evaluating the compliance, effectiveness, and efficiency of the BCMS. Audits involve systematically reviewing processes, procedures, and documentation to identify any non-conformities or areas for improvement. The results of audits help identify gaps and opportunities for enhancing the BCMS.

3. Risk Assessments: Conducting periodic risk assessments helps identify and assess potential risks to the organization's operations and critical functions. By evaluating the likelihood and impact of different risks, organizations can prioritize their mitigation efforts and allocate resources accordingly. Risk assessments provide valuable insights for improving the BCMS's risk management capabilities.

4. Incident and Business Continuity Exercise Evaluations: Evaluating the performance of incident response and business continuity exercises helps measure the readiness and effectiveness of the BCMS. By analyzing the outcomes of exercises, organizations can identify areas that require improvement, such as response time, communication effectiveness, coordination among teams, and decision-making processes.

5. Feedback and Surveys: Gathering feedback from stakeholders, including employees, customers, and partners, is an essential tool for monitoring and measuring the BCMS. Feedback can be obtained through surveys, interviews, focus groups, or suggestion systems. It provides valuable insights into stakeholder perceptions, satisfaction levels, and areas where improvements can be made.

6. Data Analysis: Analyzing relevant data related to incidents, disruptions, recovery activities, and performance can provide insights into the effectiveness of the BCMS. Data analysis techniques, such as trend analysis, statistical analysis, and root cause analysis, can help identify patterns, trends, and areas for improvement.

7. Management Review Meetings: Regular management review meetings provide a forum for evaluating the overall performance of the BCMS. These meetings involve top management and key stakeholders reviewing key performance indicators, audit findings, incident reports, and other relevant information. The discussions and decisions made during these meetings help drive improvement initiatives.

8. Software and Technology Tools: Various software and technology tools are available to support the monitoring and measurement of the BCMS. These tools can help automate data collection, analysis, reporting, and tracking of performance indicators. They provide a centralized repository for documentation, incident management, risk assessments, and communication, enhancing the efficiency and effectiveness of the monitoring and measurement process.

When selecting techniques and tools for monitoring and measuring the BCMS, organizations should consider their specific needs, resources, and objectives. It is important to choose methods that align with the organization's overall goals and allow for meaningful analysis and improvement of the BCMS.

9.4 Performance Evaluation and Analysis

How to evaluate and analyze BCMS performance data

Evaluating and analyzing Business Continuity Management System (BCMS) performance data is crucial for assessing the effectiveness of the system and identifying areas for improvement. Here are the steps to effectively evaluate and analyze BCMS performance data:

1. Identify Relevant Performance Metrics: Determine the key performance indicators (KPIs) and metrics that align with the objectives and goals of the BCMS. These metrics should be measurable, relevant, and directly linked to the organization's business continuity objectives. Common performance metrics include recovery time objectives (RTO), recovery point objectives (RPO), incident response times, testing completion rates, and customer satisfaction ratings.

2. Collect Data: Gather the necessary data related to the identified performance metrics. This can include incident reports, testing and exercise results, customer feedback, audit findings, and any other relevant information. Ensure that the data is accurate, reliable, and representative of the BCMS's performance.

3. Organize and Consolidate Data: Organize and consolidate the collected data in a structured format for ease of analysis. This can be done using spreadsheets, databases, or specialized software tools. Ensure that the data is properly labeled, categorized, and standardized to facilitate analysis.

4. Perform Data Analysis: Analyze the collected data using appropriate data analysis techniques. This may include statistical analysis, trend analysis, benchmarking, root cause analysis, or any other relevant analytical methods. Identify patterns, trends, anomalies, and areas of concern within the data.

5. Compare against Targets or Benchmarks: Compare the analyzed data against pre-established targets, benchmarks, or industry best practices. This helps evaluate the performance of the BCMS in relation to desired goals and external standards. Identify any gaps or deviations from the targets or benchmarks.

6. Identify Root Causes and Improvement Opportunities: Use the analysis results to identify root causes of any performance gaps or areas requiring improvement. Determine the underlying factors contributing to the observed patterns or trends. This may involve conducting further investigations, seeking input from relevant stakeholders, or performing more detailed analysis.

7. Generate Insights and Recommendations: Based on the analysis, generate insights and recommendations for improving the BCMS's performance. This can include identifying specific actions to address identified issues, proposing process changes, allocating resources, or revising policies and procedures. Ensure that the recommendations are actionable, realistic, and aligned with the organization's overall objectives.

8. Communicate Findings: Communicate the findings, insights, and recommendations to key stakeholders within the organization. This can be done through reports, presentations, or meetings. Clearly articulate the implications of the analysis and the potential benefits of implementing the recommended improvements.

9. Track Progress and Repeat Analysis: Monitor the implementation of improvement initiatives and track progress over time. Continuously evaluate the impact of implemented changes on the BCMS performance. Regularly repeat the data analysis process to assess ongoing performance and identify further areas for improvement.

By following these steps, organizations can effectively evaluate and analyze BCMS performance data to gain insights, make informed decisions, and drive continual improvement. It ensures that the BCMS remains aligned with business objectives, enhances resilience, and maintains the organization's ability to effectively manage potential disruptions.

Using performance data to identify opportunities for improvement

Using performance data to identify opportunities for improvement is a crucial step in driving the continual improvement of the Business Continuity Management System (BCMS). Here's how you can effectively use performance data to identify improvement opportunities:

1. Define Key Performance Indicators (KPIs): Establish clear and measurable KPIs that align with the objectives of the BCMS. These KPIs should be specific, relevant, and actionable. Examples could include recovery time objectives (RTO), testing completion rates, incident response times, or customer satisfaction ratings.

2. Collect and Analyze Performance Data: Gather relevant data related to the identified KPIs. This can include incident reports, test results, audit findings,

customer feedback, and other performance-related information. Analyze the data to identify trends, patterns, and areas of concern.

3. Compare Data Against Targets or Benchmarks: Compare the performance data against established targets or industry benchmarks. This allows you to assess how well the BCMS is performing in relation to desired goals and external standards. Identify any gaps or deviations that indicate areas for improvement.

4. Conduct Root Cause Analysis: Investigate the underlying causes of performance gaps or areas that require improvement. This involves conducting root cause analysis to identify the factors contributing to the observed performance issues. Use tools like the "5 Whys" technique or fishbone diagrams to dig deeper and identify the root causes.

5. Engage Stakeholders: Engage relevant stakeholders, including employees, customers, partners, and auditors, in the analysis and discussion of performance data. Seek their input and perspectives to gain a comprehensive understanding of the issues and potential improvement opportunities.

6. Prioritize Improvement Opportunities: Prioritize improvement opportunities based on their potential impact and alignment with organizational goals. Consider factors such as the severity of the issue, the feasibility of implementing improvements, and the resources required. Focus on areas that offer the greatest potential for enhancing the effectiveness and resilience of the BCMS.

7. Develop Improvement Plans: Develop action plans to address the identified improvement opportunities. Define specific goals, actions, timelines, and responsible individuals or teams. Ensure that the improvement plans are realistic, achievable, and aligned with the organization's overall strategy and resources.

8. Implement and Monitor Improvement Initiatives: Execute the improvement plans and closely monitor the progress and outcomes of the initiatives. Regularly review the effectiveness of the implemented improvements and assess their impact on the BCMS performance. Adjust the plans as necessary based on feedback and evolving needs.

9. Communicate and Share Learnings: Communicate the improvement initiatives and their outcomes to relevant stakeholders. Share the learnings and best practices with the organization to promote a culture of continuous improvement. Document and disseminate the success stories, challenges, and lessons learned to foster knowledge sharing and encourage further improvements.

By effectively using performance data to identify improvement opportunities, organizations can drive the continual enhancement of their BCMS. This ensures that the system remains robust, adaptable, and aligned with business objectives, enabling the organization to effectively manage disruptions and ensure business continuity.

9.5 Addressing Non-conformities and Corrective Actions

Understanding the concept of non-conformities in BCMS

- In the context of the Business Continuity Management System (BCMS), non-conformities refer to instances where the BCMS does not meet the requirements set forth by the relevant standards, regulations, or internal policies and procedures. Non-conformities can arise from various sources, including gaps in processes, documentation, training, or implementation of controls.

- Non-conformities can be identified through various means, such as internal audits, external assessments, incident investigations, or customer feedback. They can manifest as deviations from documented procedures, inadequate risk mitigation measures, deficiencies in training or awareness, or failures to meet regulatory requirements.

- Non-conformities can be classified into different categories based on their severity and impact on the BCMS and business operations. These categories may include minor non-conformities, major non-conformities, and critical non-conformities. The severity of a non-conformity depends on factors such as the potential impact on business continuity, legal and regulatory compliance, customer satisfaction, or the organization's reputation.

- When a non-conformity is identified, it is essential to take appropriate corrective actions to address the root causes and prevent its recurrence. The corrective actions may include process improvements, revisions to documentation, training or awareness programs, or the implementation of additional controls. The goal is to rectify the non-conformity, mitigate any potential risks or impacts, and ensure that the BCMS aligns with the required standards and objectives.

- It is crucial to have a systematic approach for managing non-conformities within the BCMS. This typically involves documenting the non-conformity, conducting an investigation to determine the root cause, developing and implementing corrective actions, and monitoring their effectiveness. The organization should establish clear responsibilities and timelines for addressing non-conformities and track their resolution to closure.

- By effectively addressing non-conformities in the BCMS, organizations can strengthen their business continuity capabilities, enhance compliance with relevant standards, and improve overall operational resilience. Continuous monitoring, assessment, and improvement of the BCMS help prevent non-conformities and foster a culture of excellence in business continuity management.

Steps to address non-conformities and take corrective actions

When non-conformities are identified within the Business Continuity Management System (BCMS), it is important to take prompt corrective actions to address the issues and prevent their recurrence. Here are the steps to address non-conformities and take corrective actions:

1. Identify and Document the Non-Conformity: Clearly identify and document the non-conformity, describing the specific area or process where the non-conformity exists. Provide details on the nature of the non-conformity and any associated evidence or supporting information.

2. Investigate the Root Cause: Conduct a thorough investigation to determine the root cause of the non-conformity. Use techniques such as root cause analysis, the "5 Whys," or fishbone diagrams to identify the underlying factors or systemic issues that contributed to the non-conformity. Seek input from relevant stakeholders to gather insights and perspectives.

3. Develop Corrective Actions: Based on the findings of the root cause analysis, develop appropriate corrective actions to address the non-conformity. Ensure that the corrective actions directly target the root cause and are feasible, realistic, and aligned with the organization's resources and capabilities. Consider preventive actions that can help mitigate similar non-conformities in the future.

4. Determine Responsibility and Assign Accountability: Assign responsibility for implementing the corrective actions to individuals or teams within the organization. Clearly define their roles and responsibilities, and ensure they have the necessary authority, resources, and expertise to execute the corrective actions effectively.

5. Establish Timelines and Action Plans: Define specific timelines and action plans for implementing the corrective actions. Establish milestones and checkpoints to monitor progress and ensure that the actions are completed within the agreed-upon timeframe. Regularly communicate the timelines and action plans to relevant stakeholders.

6. Implement Corrective Actions: Execute the corrective actions according to the defined action plans. Monitor the progress of implementation and provide support as needed. Ensure that the corrective actions address the root cause of the non-conformity and align with the requirements of the BCMS.

7. Monitor and Verify Effectiveness: Monitor the effectiveness of the implemented corrective actions through ongoing monitoring, measurement, and performance evaluation. Verify that the actions have successfully resolved the non-conformity and are preventing its recurrence. Collect and analyze data to assess the impact of the corrective actions.

8. Document and Communicate: Document all actions taken to address the non-conformity, including the implemented corrective actions and their outcomes. Update relevant documentation, such as procedures, policies, or work instructions, as necessary. Communicate the resolution of the non-conformity to stakeholders, ensuring transparency and accountability.

9. Review and Close: Review the effectiveness of the corrective actions and assess whether the non-conformity has been adequately addressed. Verify that the BCMS now conforms to the required standards or requirements. Once the

non-conformity is resolved, close the non-conformity record and update the status accordingly.

10. Learn and Improve: Capture lessons learned from the non-conformity and the corrective action process. Share these lessons with relevant stakeholders to improve the effectiveness of the BCMS. Use the insights gained to enhance processes, procedures, training, and overall business continuity practices.

By following these steps, organizations can effectively address non-conformities within the BCMS and implement corrective actions to improve performance, enhance compliance, and strengthen the organization's overall business continuity capabilities.

9.6 Regular Review and Update of the BCMS

The necessity for regular reviews and updates of the BCMS

Regular reviews and updates of the Business Continuity Management System (BCMS) are essential to ensure its effectiveness, alignment with organizational objectives, and continued relevance in the face of evolving risks and requirements. Here are the key reasons why regular reviews and updates of the BCMS are necessary:

1. Adaptation to Changing Context: The business environment is dynamic, and organizations face ever-changing risks, regulations, technologies, and customer expectations. Regular reviews allow organizations to assess the current context in which the BCMS operates and make necessary adjustments to ensure its alignment with the evolving business landscape.

2. Identification of Improvement Opportunities: Through regular reviews, organizations can identify improvement opportunities within the BCMS. Reviews help identify areas where the BCMS may be falling short or not fully meeting objectives, allowing organizations to take corrective actions and drive continual improvement.

3. Compliance with Standards and Regulations: Regulatory requirements, industry standards, and best practices evolve over time. Regular reviews help organizations ensure that the BCMS remains compliant with the latest standards and regulations, reducing the risk of non-compliance and associated penalties.

4. Enhanced Risk Management: Regular reviews of the BCMS enable organizations to evaluate the effectiveness of risk mitigation measures and identify emerging risks. This allows for proactive adjustments to the BCMS to address emerging threats and enhance risk management practices.

5. Stakeholder Engagement and Alignment: Regular reviews provide an opportunity to engage with stakeholders, including employees, customers, suppliers, and regulators. By involving stakeholders in the review process, organizations can gather valuable input and ensure alignment between the BCMS and stakeholder expectations.

6. Organizational Learning: Regular reviews facilitate organizational learning by capturing lessons from incidents, exercises, audits, and other feedback mechanisms. This enables organizations to leverage insights gained from past experiences to enhance the BCMS and improve resilience.

7. Continuous Improvement: The goal of regular reviews and updates is to drive continuous improvement within the BCMS. By identifying areas for enhancement and implementing necessary changes, organizations can strengthen their business continuity capabilities and achieve a higher level of readiness.

To ensure the effectiveness of reviews and updates, organizations should establish a structured process for conducting periodic assessments, define roles and responsibilities, set clear objectives, and allocate appropriate resources. It is important to document the findings, actions, and outcomes of the reviews and communicate them to relevant stakeholders.

By regularly reviewing and updating the BCMS, organizations demonstrate their commitment to business continuity, maintain compliance, enhance resilience, and foster a culture of continual improvement. This enables them to effectively respond to disruptions, protect their operations, and ensure the ongoing provision of products and services to customers.

How to conduct a systematic review and update of the BCMS

Conducting a systematic review and update of the Business Continuity Management System (BCMS) ensures its ongoing effectiveness and alignment with organizational objectives. Here are the steps to conduct a systematic review and update of the BCMS:

1. Establish Review Objectives: Clearly define the objectives of the review, such as assessing the overall performance of the BCMS, identifying areas for improvement, ensuring compliance with standards and regulations, or addressing specific organizational priorities. These objectives will guide the review process.

2. Review Documentation: Start by reviewing the existing documentation of the BCMS, including policies, procedures, plans, and records. Evaluate their completeness, accuracy, and relevance. Identify any gaps, inconsistencies, or outdated information that require updates.

3. Collect Feedback and Input: Engage with relevant stakeholders, including employees, management, customers, and external partners, to gather feedback on the BCMS's effectiveness. Conduct interviews, surveys, or workshops to obtain insights, perspectives, and suggestions for improvement. Consider incorporating lessons learned from incidents, exercises, and audits.

4. Evaluate Performance Against Objectives: Assess the performance of the BCMS against its defined objectives, targets, and key performance indicators (KPIs). Analyze data and metrics related to incident response, recovery capabilities, testing outcomes, and other relevant factors. Identify areas of success and areas that require improvement.

5. Conduct Gap Analysis: Compare the current state of the BCMS with desired outcomes, industry best practices, and relevant standards or regulations. Identify any gaps, deficiencies, or areas where the BCMS does not meet the intended requirements or expectations. This analysis helps prioritize areas for improvement.

6. Identify Improvement Opportunities: Based on the gap analysis and feedback gathered, identify specific improvement opportunities for the BCMS. This could involve updating policies and procedures, enhancing training programs, refining risk assessments, strengthening recovery strategies, or improving communication processes. Ensure that improvement opportunities align with organizational goals and priorities.

7. Develop an Update Plan: Create a detailed plan outlining the necessary updates and improvements to the BCMS. Define specific actions, responsibilities, timelines, and resources required for each update. Prioritize the updates based on their impact, feasibility, and urgency. Obtain necessary approvals and allocate appropriate resources to support the update plan.

8. Implement Updates: Execute the update plan by implementing the identified improvements. This may involve revising policies and procedures, updating documentation, conducting additional training, enhancing communication channels, or implementing new technologies. Ensure that the updates are effectively communicated to relevant stakeholders and integrated into daily operations.

9. Monitor and Measure Effectiveness: Monitor the implementation of the updates and measure their effectiveness. Collect relevant data and metrics to assess the impact of the improvements on the BCMS's performance. Continuously monitor the progress and gather feedback to evaluate the effectiveness of the updates.

10. Document and Communicate: Document the updates made to the BCMS, including revised policies, procedures, and other relevant documentation. Communicate the updates and their rationale to all stakeholders involved in the BCMS. Provide appropriate training and awareness programs to ensure understanding and compliance with the updated processes.

11. Establish a Review Cycle: Establish a regular review cycle for the BCMS to ensure its ongoing effectiveness. Define the frequency of future reviews, taking into account the organization's specific needs, industry requirements, and the rate of change in the business environment. Document the review cycle in the BCMS documentation.

By following these steps, organizations can conduct a systematic review and update of the BCMS, ensuring its continued relevance, effectiveness, and alignment with organizational objectives. This promotes resilience, enhances business continuity capabilities, and enables organizations to proactively address emerging risks and challenges.

9.7 Role of Innovation in BCMS Improvement

How innovation can drive improvements in the BCMS

Innovation plays a crucial role in driving improvements in the Business Continuity Management System (BCMS). By embracing innovative approaches, organizations can enhance their business continuity capabilities, strengthen their resilience, and effectively respond to evolving challenges. Here are some ways in which innovation can drive improvements in the BCMS:

1. Technology Adoption: Embracing innovative technologies can significantly enhance the efficiency and effectiveness of the BCMS. Automation tools, data analytics, cloud computing, artificial intelligence, and machine learning can streamline processes, improve data management, enable faster decision-making, and enhance incident response capabilities. Organizations can leverage technology to automate business continuity planning, conduct real-time monitoring, and facilitate effective communication during disruptions.

2. Integrated Systems: Integrating the BCMS with other management systems, such as quality management or environmental management, can lead to synergies and efficiencies. By aligning and integrating processes, organizations can optimize resources, reduce duplication, and improve overall performance. This integration can drive improvements in risk management, incident response, and organizational resilience.

3. Agile Planning and Adaptive Strategies: Innovation can enable organizations to adopt more agile planning methodologies and adaptive strategies. By embracing innovative approaches such as agile project management or design thinking, organizations can respond quickly to changing circumstances, identify emerging risks, and develop more effective and flexible business continuity strategies. This iterative approach allows organizations to continuously learn and improve their response capabilities.

4. Collaboration and Knowledge Sharing: Innovation can foster collaboration and knowledge sharing among stakeholders within and outside the organization. Utilizing collaboration platforms, social networks, and other innovative tools, organizations can connect employees, partners, and customers to share insights, best practices, lessons learned, and innovative ideas related to business continuity. This collective intelligence can drive continuous improvement in the BCMS.

5. Scenario Planning and Simulations: Innovation can enhance scenario planning and simulation exercises. Advanced modeling, simulation tools, and virtual reality can help organizations simulate various disruptive scenarios, test the effectiveness of response strategies, and identify areas for improvement. By embracing innovative simulation techniques, organizations can refine their response plans, train personnel, and enhance decision-making under simulated crisis situations.

6. Continuous Monitoring and Data Analytics: Innovation can enable organizations to adopt real-time monitoring systems and data analytics tools to detect early warning signals, monitor key performance indicators, and

identify potential risks or vulnerabilities. By leveraging big data analytics, organizations can gain insights from vast amounts of data to enhance situational awareness, improve risk assessments, and make data-driven decisions for proactive risk management and continuous improvement.

7. Stakeholder Engagement: Innovative approaches can enhance stakeholder engagement in the BCMS. Using digital platforms, organizations can engage stakeholders in the business continuity planning process, seek their feedback, and involve them in exercises and drills. This collaborative approach ensures that diverse perspectives are considered, leading to more effective and comprehensive business continuity strategies.

8. Learning and Adaptation: Innovation can foster a culture of learning and adaptation within the organization. By encouraging experimentation, embracing failure as an opportunity for growth, and promoting a mindset of continuous improvement, organizations can harness innovation to drive positive change in the BCMS. Creating avenues for employees to share innovative ideas and rewarding innovative thinking can motivate employees to contribute to the improvement of the BCMS.

Incorporating innovation into the BCMS allows organizations to stay ahead of evolving risks, exploit new opportunities, and continuously improve their resilience. By embracing technological advancements, fostering collaboration, promoting adaptive planning, and leveraging data-driven insights, organizations can drive significant improvements in their BCMS, ensuring the organization's ability to effectively manage disruptions and maintain business continuity.

Strategies for fostering a culture of innovation in BCMS management

Fostering a culture of innovation in Business Continuity Management System (BCMS) management is crucial for driving continuous improvement and enhancing organizational resilience. Here are some strategies to cultivate a culture of innovation in BCMS management:

1. Leadership Support: Leadership plays a vital role in fostering a culture of innovation. Leaders should actively support and promote innovation in the BCMS. They should communicate the importance of innovation, allocate resources for innovative initiatives, and lead by example through their own innovative behaviors.

2. Encourage Risk-Taking and Learning: Create a safe environment where employees are encouraged to take calculated risks and learn from failures. Encourage employees to think creatively, challenge existing practices, and experiment with new ideas. Emphasize that failure is an opportunity for learning and improvement, fostering a growth mindset within the organization.

3. Open Communication and Collaboration: Foster an open and collaborative culture where ideas and knowledge can be freely shared. Establish channels for open communication and encourage cross-functional collaboration. Encourage

employees to collaborate on innovative projects, share insights, and provide feedback to drive collective innovation in BCMS management.

4. Provide Resources and Support: Allocate resources, including time, budget, and technology, to support innovative initiatives within the BCMS. Provide employees with the necessary training, tools, and access to information to foster innovation. Support innovation through dedicated innovation teams, innovation labs, or designated roles responsible for driving innovation in BCMS management.

5. Reward and Recognize Innovation: Recognize and reward employees who contribute to innovation in BCMS management. Establish reward systems that acknowledge innovative ideas, successful implementations, and continuous improvement efforts. This recognition can motivate employees to actively participate in innovation initiatives and create a positive culture around innovation.

6. Embrace Technology and Automation: Embrace technology and automation to streamline BCMS processes and drive innovation. Explore innovative software solutions, digital platforms, and data analytics tools that can enhance the efficiency and effectiveness of BCMS management. Encourage employees to leverage technology and explore innovative solutions to improve business continuity practices.

7. Encourage Continuous Learning: Promote a culture of continuous learning within the organization. Provide opportunities for employees to enhance their knowledge and skills related to business continuity management. Encourage employees to attend training programs, workshops, industry conferences, and participate in professional development activities to stay updated with the latest trends and practices.

8. Learn from External Sources: Look for inspiration and ideas from external sources such as industry best practices, case studies, and benchmarking exercises. Encourage employees to stay informed about emerging trends, research findings, and innovative practices in BCMS management. Incorporate external insights into the organization's approach to drive innovation.

9. Establish Innovation Metrics: Define and measure innovation metrics specific to BCMS management. This could include metrics related to the number of innovative ideas generated, successful implementation of innovative initiatives, impact on improving BCMS effectiveness, or cost savings achieved through innovation. Regularly assess and monitor these metrics to gauge the progress and impact of innovation efforts.

10. Continual Improvement Mindset: Instill a mindset of continual improvement in BCMS management. Encourage employees to constantly seek ways to improve processes, systems, and practices related to business continuity. Emphasize the importance of innovation as a key driver of continual improvement and resilience.

By implementing these strategies, organizations can foster a culture of innovation in BCMS management, driving continuous improvement, and enhancing their ability to effectively respond to disruptions and maintain business continuity.

9.8 Maintaining Readiness and Resilience

The significance of maintaining readiness and resilience in BCMS

Maintaining readiness and resilience in the Business Continuity Management System (BCMS) is of utmost importance to ensure an organization's ability to effectively respond to and recover from disruptions. Here are the key reasons why maintaining readiness and resilience in BCMS is significant:

1. Timely Response to Disruptions: Readiness and resilience enable organizations to respond promptly to disruptions, minimizing their impact on business operations. By having well-defined plans, trained personnel, and tested response procedures in place, organizations can quickly mobilize resources, activate recovery strategies, and mitigate the negative consequences of disruptions.

2. Minimized Downtime and Financial Loss: A resilient BCMS helps minimize downtime and financial losses during disruptions. By maintaining readiness, organizations can identify critical functions, prioritize recovery efforts, and implement efficient recovery measures. This reduces the duration and severity of business interruptions, enabling faster restoration of operations and reducing the financial impact on the organization.

3. Protection of Reputation and Stakeholder Confidence: Maintaining readiness and resilience in BCMS safeguards an organization's reputation and instills confidence in stakeholders. Effective response and recovery measures demonstrate an organization's commitment to business continuity, customer service, and stakeholder welfare. This builds trust and enhances the organization's reputation, reducing the potential negative impact on customer relationships, brand image, and market perception.

4. Compliance with Regulatory Requirements: Readiness and resilience in BCMS ensure compliance with regulatory requirements and industry standards. Many sectors have regulations that mandate organizations to have robust business continuity plans in place. By maintaining readiness and resilience, organizations can demonstrate compliance, avoiding legal or regulatory penalties, and maintaining the trust of regulators, customers, and partners.

5. Preservation of Competitive Advantage: Maintaining a resilient BCMS provides a competitive advantage in the marketplace. Organizations that can maintain operations during disruptions and recover swiftly gain a competitive edge over their counterparts. They can fulfill customer commitments, meet service level agreements, and retain clients even in challenging circumstances, positioning themselves as reliable and trustworthy partners.

6. Employee Safety and Well-being: Readiness and resilience in BCMS prioritize employee safety and well-being during disruptions. By having well-defined emergency response plans, communication protocols, and evacuation

procedures, organizations can protect their employees from harm and provide a safe working environment. This enhances employee morale, loyalty, and retention.

7. Continuous Improvement: Maintaining readiness and resilience involves ongoing assessment, testing, and updating of the BCMS. This process promotes a culture of continual improvement, enabling organizations to identify weaknesses, address gaps, and enhance their business continuity capabilities over time. It ensures that the BCMS remains relevant, effective, and aligned with changing risks and organizational needs.

8. Enhanced Organizational Resilience: Readiness and resilience in BCMS contribute to the overall resilience of an organization. Resilience is the ability to absorb shocks, adapt to changes, and quickly recover from disruptions. By maintaining readiness, organizations build a solid foundation for resilience, enabling them to navigate uncertainties, adapt to evolving circumstances, and emerge stronger from disruptions.

In summary, maintaining readiness and resilience in the BCMS is essential for organizations to effectively respond to disruptions, minimize financial losses, protect reputation, comply with regulations, preserve competitive advantage, prioritize employee safety, foster a culture of continuous improvement, and enhance overall organizational resilience. By investing in maintaining readiness, organizations can better prepare for uncertainties and safeguard their long-term success.

Tactics for ensuring the organization is always prepared and resilient

Ensuring that an organization is always prepared and resilient requires a proactive approach and the implementation of various tactics. Here are some tactics to consider:

1. Risk Assessment and Scenario Planning: Conduct regular risk assessments to identify potential threats and vulnerabilities. This includes analyzing internal and external factors that could impact the organization's operations. Scenario planning helps anticipate various disruptions and develop response strategies in advance.

2. Robust Business Continuity Planning: Develop comprehensive business continuity plans (BCPs) that outline clear response and recovery procedures for different types of disruptions. These plans should address key areas such as communication, employee safety, IT systems, supply chain, and critical business functions. Regularly review and update the BCPs to ensure their effectiveness.

3. Training and Awareness Programs: Provide regular training to employees on business continuity protocols, response procedures, and their roles and responsibilities during disruptions. Conduct drills and exercises to test the effectiveness of the plans and enhance employee preparedness. Foster a culture of awareness and accountability throughout the organization.

4. Regular Testing and Exercising: Perform routine tests and exercises to evaluate the readiness and effectiveness of the BCMS. This includes tabletop exercises, functional drills, and full-scale simulations. Assess the organization's ability to execute the BCPs, identify areas for improvement, and make necessary adjustments.

5. Continuous Monitoring and Reporting: Implement a robust monitoring system to track key performance indicators (KPIs) related to the BCMS. Monitor early warning signs and emerging risks to enable timely response. Establish reporting mechanisms to capture incidents, near misses, and lessons learned. Regularly analyze the data to identify trends, evaluate performance, and drive improvements.

6. Engage Stakeholders: Foster strong relationships with key stakeholders such as customers, suppliers, regulators, and industry peers. Collaborate on risk management, share best practices, and establish mutual support mechanisms. Engage stakeholders in the development and testing of the BCMS to ensure a coordinated and integrated approach.

7. Technology and Automation: Leverage technological tools and automation to enhance preparedness and resilience. Implement business continuity management software to streamline documentation, communication, and incident response. Utilize real-time monitoring systems, predictive analytics, and automation tools to detect and respond to disruptions more effectively.

8. Supplier and Vendor Management: Assess and monitor the resilience of critical suppliers and vendors. Establish backup plans and alternative sources to mitigate risks associated with supply chain disruptions. Maintain regular communication and conduct joint exercises to ensure alignment in business continuity strategies.

9. Post-Incident Evaluation and Learning: Conduct thorough evaluations after each incident or disruption to identify lessons learned and areas for improvement. Capture feedback from employees, stakeholders, and customers. Use this feedback to refine the BCMS, update policies and procedures, and enhance preparedness for future events.

10. Leadership Commitment and Communication: Ensure that leadership demonstrates commitment to preparedness and resilience. Communicate the importance of business continuity to all levels of the organization. Establish clear roles and responsibilities for BCMS implementation. Provide resources and support for continuous improvement initiatives.

By implementing these tactics, organizations can enhance their preparedness and resilience, enabling them to effectively navigate disruptions and ensure continuity of operations. It is an ongoing process that requires continuous monitoring, evaluation, and adaptation to changing circumstances.

9.9 Summary

Recap of the concepts, methods, and strategies for maintaining and improving the BCMS

In summary, maintaining and improving the Business Continuity Management System (BCMS) is a critical aspect of ensuring organizational resilience and readiness to handle disruptions. Throughout Chapter 9, we explored various concepts, methods, and strategies to achieve this. Here's a recap of the key points covered:

1. Continuous Improvement: We emphasized the importance of embracing a culture of continuous improvement in the BCMS. By constantly monitoring, evaluating, and refining the system, organizations can enhance their preparedness and response capabilities.

2. Monitoring and Measurement: Regular monitoring and measurement of BCMS performance are crucial for assessing effectiveness and identifying areas for improvement. Utilizing tools and techniques such as data analytics and performance metrics enables organizations to track progress and make data-driven decisions.

3. Non-Conformities and Corrective Actions: Non-conformities are deviations from the desired BCMS performance. We discussed the significance of addressing non-conformities promptly and implementing corrective actions to prevent their recurrence.

4. Review and Update: Regular reviews and updates of the BCMS are necessary to ensure its continued relevance and effectiveness. By considering changes in the organizational context, emerging risks, and lessons learned, organizations can make informed updates and adjustments.

5. Innovation and Technology: Innovation plays a vital role in BCMS maintenance and improvement. By leveraging technology, organizations can streamline processes, enhance data management, and drive innovation in areas such as scenario planning, simulation, and automation.

6. Training, Awareness, and Competence: Building a skilled and knowledgeable workforce through training programs and awareness initiatives is crucial for maintaining an effective BCMS. Continuous development of competencies ensures that personnel can effectively contribute to the system's improvement.

7. Internal Audit and Management Review: Conducting internal audits and management reviews are integral components of maintaining and improving the BCMS. These processes help identify areas of strength and weakness, validate compliance with standards, and drive continuous improvement.

8. Resource Allocation: Adequate allocation of resources, including human, technological, financial, and physical resources, is essential for sustaining and improving the BCMS. Organizations must prioritize resource allocation based on risk assessments and business continuity priorities.

9. Readiness and Resilience: We discussed the significance of maintaining readiness and resilience in the BCMS. By proactively identifying risks, developing robust plans, and regularly testing and updating procedures, organizations can enhance their ability to respond to disruptions.

10. Culture of Preparedness: Establishing a culture of preparedness throughout the organization is crucial. This includes fostering leadership commitment, promoting open communication, encouraging employee engagement, and aligning BCMS objectives with the organization's overall goals.

By incorporating these concepts, methods, and strategies into the BCMS, organizations can continuously maintain and improve their resilience and readiness. It is an ongoing process that requires commitment, collaboration, and a proactive approach to effectively manage disruptions and ensure the organization's long-term success.

Preparing for the next stage: external audits and ISO 22301 certification

- Chapter 10: External Audits and ISO 22301 Certification 10.1 Introduction • Understanding the role of external audits and certification in validating BCMS compliance with ISO 22301

- 10.2 The Purpose and Benefits of External Audits • Exploring the purpose and benefits of external audits in the context of ISO 22301 certification • Highlighting the importance of independent verification and validation of BCMS

- 10.3 Selecting an Accredited Certification Body • Guidelines for selecting a reputable and accredited certification body for ISO 22301 certification • Considering factors such as expertise, reputation, and industry recognition

- 10.4 Preparing for an External Audit • Steps to prepare for an external audit, including documentation review, process assessment, and readiness checks • Ensuring alignment with ISO 22301 requirements and addressing any identified gaps

- 10.5 The External Audit Process • Overview of the external audit process, including initial audit planning, on-site assessments, and interviews with relevant personnel • Understanding the roles and responsibilities of auditors and auditees during the audit process

- 10.6 Handling Audit Findings and Non-Conformities • Steps to manage and address audit findings and non-conformities identified during the external audit • Implementing corrective actions and establishing effective preventive measures

- 10.7 Achieving ISO 22301 Certification • Understanding the requirements and process for obtaining ISO 22301 certification • Preparing the necessary documentation, completing the certification application, and scheduling the certification audit

☐ 10.8 Maintaining ISO 22301 Certification • The ongoing commitment and activities required to maintain ISO 22301 certification • Conducting regular internal audits, management reviews, and surveillance audits to ensure ongoing compliance

☐ 10.9 Benefits of ISO 22301 Certification • Exploring the benefits and advantages of ISO 22301 certification for organizations • Enhanced credibility, competitive advantage, and increased stakeholder confidence

☐ 10.10 Integrating ISO 22301 Certification with Other Management Systems • Understanding the potential for integration with other ISO management system standards • Exploring the benefits and synergies of implementing multiple management systems

☐ 10.11 Summary • Recap of the external audit and ISO 22301 certification process • Highlighting the significance of independent validation and ongoing compliance with the standard

This chapter will include case studies, practical exercises, and tips to guide readers in maintaining and improving their organization's BCMS in accordance with ISO 22301.

CHAPTER 10

External Audits and ISO 22301 Certification

10.1 Introduction

Understanding the role and significance of external audits and ISO 22301 certification

External audits and ISO 22301 certification play a crucial role in validating the compliance and effectiveness of a Business Continuity Management System (BCMS) based on ISO 22301. Here's an overview of their role and significance:

1. Validation of Compliance: External audits assess the organization's BCMS against the requirements of ISO 22301. They provide an independent and objective evaluation of the system's compliance with the standard. Auditors review documentation, processes, and practices to ensure alignment with ISO 22301, identifying any non-conformities or areas for improvement.

2. Independent Verification: External audits provide an external perspective on the effectiveness of the BCMS. They offer an unbiased assessment, verifying that the organization has implemented and maintained the necessary controls, procedures, and measures to ensure business continuity. This verification builds confidence among stakeholders and enhances the credibility of the organization.

3. Identification of Gaps and Improvement Opportunities: Through the audit process, external auditors may identify gaps, weaknesses, or non-conformities in the BCMS. These findings help the organization identify areas for improvement and take corrective actions. The audit process serves as a valuable feedback mechanism to enhance the effectiveness and resilience of the BCMS.

4. Compliance with Industry Standards and Regulations: ISO 22301 certification demonstrates that an organization has met the internationally recognized standards for business continuity management. Certification provides assurance to stakeholders, customers, and partners that the organization has implemented a robust BCMS. It also helps meet regulatory requirements in sectors where ISO 22301 certification is mandated or preferred.

5. Competitive Advantage: ISO 22301 certification can provide a competitive edge in the market. It showcases the organization's commitment to business continuity and risk management, differentiating it from competitors. Certification may be a requirement for participating in certain contracts or business opportunities, giving certified organizations a competitive advantage in bidding processes.

6. **Increased Stakeholder Confidence:** ISO 22301 certification instills confidence in stakeholders, including customers, investors, regulators, and business partners. It demonstrates the organization's proactive approach to risk management and its ability to ensure continuity of critical operations. Certification builds trust and strengthens relationships with stakeholders, fostering long-term partnerships and customer loyalty.

7. **Integration with Management Systems:** ISO 22301 certification can be integrated with other management system certifications, such as ISO 9001 (Quality Management System) or ISO 14001 (Environmental Management System). This integration streamlines processes, reduces duplication, and enhances the overall effectiveness of the organization's management systems.

8. **Continual Improvement:** External audits and ISO 22301 certification encourage organizations to embrace a culture of continual improvement. They provide feedback on the effectiveness of the BCMS, driving organizations to identify areas for enhancement and implement corrective actions. Certification serves as a catalyst for ongoing improvement, ensuring the BCMS remains robust and aligned with evolving risks and business needs.

In summary, external audits and ISO 22301 certification play a vital role in validating the compliance, effectiveness, and resilience of a BCMS. They provide independent verification, identify improvement opportunities, enhance stakeholder confidence, and contribute to the organization's competitive advantage. By achieving and maintaining ISO 22301 certification, organizations demonstrate their commitment to business continuity and risk management, positioning themselves as resilient and trustworthy partners in the marketplace.

10.2 Preparing for an External Audit

Steps for preparing your organization for an external audit

Preparing your organization for an external audit is crucial to ensure a smooth and successful audit process. Here are the steps to consider when preparing for an external audit:

1. **Understand the Audit Scope:** Gain a clear understanding of the scope of the external audit. Review the requirements of ISO 22301 and assess which areas of your BCMS will be evaluated during the audit.

2. **Review Documentation:** Ensure that your BCMS documentation is complete, up-to-date, and easily accessible. Review policies, procedures, guidelines, and records related to business continuity. Verify that they align with ISO 22301 requirements and reflect the current state of your BCMS.

3. **Conduct a Gap Analysis:** Perform a thorough gap analysis to identify any areas of non-conformance or gaps between your current practices and the requirements of ISO 22301. Address these gaps by implementing corrective actions and making necessary improvements before the audit.

4. **Internal Audits:** Conduct internal audits of your BCMS to identify and address any non-conformities or areas for improvement. Ensure that the internal audit

process is robust and comprehensive, covering all relevant aspects of the BCMS. Implement corrective actions based on the findings of internal audits.

5. Train Employees: Provide training and awareness programs to employees regarding the BCMS and ISO 22301 requirements. Ensure that employees understand their roles and responsibilities related to business continuity. Conduct training sessions on topics such as emergency response, incident management, and recovery procedures.

6. Establish Readiness Checks: Perform readiness checks to evaluate the preparedness of your organization for the external audit. Review the key elements of the BCMS, including risk assessments, business impact analyses, recovery plans, and testing and exercising activities. Address any deficiencies or gaps identified during the readiness checks.

7. Assign Responsibility: Assign individuals or a team responsible for managing the external audit process. Clearly define their roles and responsibilities, including coordinating with the external auditors, gathering documentation, scheduling interviews, and facilitating on-site assessments.

8. Communication and Coordination: Communicate with relevant stakeholders about the upcoming external audit. Inform employees, managers, and key personnel about the audit objectives, scope, and timelines. Coordinate with different departments to ensure smooth collaboration during the audit process.

9. Conduct Mock Audits: Perform mock audits or practice sessions to simulate the external audit process. This allows your organization to identify any weaknesses, practice responding to auditor inquiries, and familiarize key personnel with the audit process. Use the feedback from mock audits to refine your BCMS and address any gaps.

10. Continuous Improvement: Continuously improve your BCMS based on lessons learned from previous audits, internal assessments, and industry best practices. Embrace a culture of continual improvement to enhance the effectiveness and resilience of your BCMS.

By following these steps, your organization can be well-prepared for an external audit, demonstrating compliance with ISO 22301 and ensuring a successful audit process.

How to choose a credible certification body

Choosing a credible certification body is crucial to ensure the integrity and validity of your ISO 22301 certification. Here are some factors to consider when selecting a certification body:

1. Accreditation: Look for certification bodies that are accredited by internationally recognized accreditation bodies. Accreditation ensures that the certification body operates according to established standards and guidelines. It provides assurance that the certification process is conducted with competence, impartiality, and integrity. Check if the certification body is

accredited by a reputable accreditation body such as ANSI, UKAS, JAS-ANZ, or DAkkS.

2. **Expertise and Experience:** Evaluate the expertise and experience of the certification body in the field of business continuity management. Consider their track record in conducting ISO 22301 certifications and their familiarity with the specific industry or sector in which your organization operates. Look for certification bodies that have a team of qualified auditors with relevant experience and expertise in business continuity management.

3. **Reputation and References:** Research the reputation of the certification body in the industry. Seek recommendations and references from organizations that have previously obtained ISO 22301 certification through the certification body. Consider feedback and testimonials from their clients to gauge their performance and professionalism.

4. **Recognition:** Check if the certification body is internationally recognized and accepted. Consider whether the certification issued by the body will be widely recognized and accepted by your stakeholders, customers, and regulatory bodies. International recognition provides credibility and ensures the validity of your ISO 22301 certification.

5. **Audit Process:** Understand the certification body's audit process and methodology. Assess their approach to conducting audits, including the level of detail and rigor they apply. Consider whether their audit process aligns with your organization's expectations and requirements. Ensure that their audit process adheres to the requirements of ISO 22301 and provides value-added insights to help improve your BCMS.

6. **Cost:** Compare the costs associated with the certification process. Request quotes from multiple certification bodies and evaluate the value for money they provide. Consider not only the initial certification costs but also any ongoing fees for surveillance audits or recertification. Ensure that the costs are transparent and aligned with the services provided.

7. **Customer Support and Services:** Evaluate the level of customer support and services offered by the certification body. Consider their responsiveness to inquiries, their availability for support during the certification process, and their ability to provide guidance and assistance when needed.

8. **Impartiality and Confidentiality:** Ensure that the certification body maintains impartiality and confidentiality throughout the certification process. Verify that they have established processes and safeguards to prevent conflicts of interest and protect the confidentiality of your organization's information.

9. **Continuous Improvement:** Assess whether the certification body demonstrates a commitment to continuous improvement. Look for certification bodies that invest in the professional development of their auditors and actively participate in industry forums and working groups to stay up-to-date with best practices.

10. **Additional Services:** Consider whether the certification body offers additional services that align with your organization's needs. This could include training

programs, workshops, or other consultancy services related to business continuity management.

By considering these factors and conducting thorough research, you can choose a credible certification body that will provide a reliable and respected ISO 22301 certification for your organization.

10.3 The External Audit Process

An overview of the external audit process

The external audit process is an important step in validating the compliance and effectiveness of a Business Continuity Management System (BCMS) against ISO 22301. Here is an overview of the typical external audit process:

1. Audit Planning: The certification body and your organization will collaborate to plan the audit. This includes determining the audit scope, objectives, timelines, and resource requirements. The certification body will request relevant documentation and information to review before the audit.

2. Opening Meeting: The external audit usually begins with an opening meeting. This meeting involves the auditors, key personnel from your organization, and any other relevant stakeholders. The auditors will explain the audit process, discuss the audit scope, and clarify expectations.

3. Document Review: The auditors will review the documentation provided by your organization, such as policies, procedures, plans, records, and evidence of implementation. They will assess the documentation for compliance with the requirements of ISO 22301 and identify any areas of non-conformance.

4. On-Site Assessments: The auditors will conduct on-site assessments to evaluate the implementation of your BCMS. They will observe processes, interview personnel, and gather evidence to verify the effectiveness and suitability of your BCMS controls, risk management practices, and continuity plans.

5. Interviews: The auditors will conduct interviews with relevant personnel across different levels and functions within your organization. These interviews aim to gather information about the understanding and implementation of the BCMS, as well as to verify the effectiveness of the controls in place.

6. Non-Conformities and Findings: During the audit, the auditors may identify non-conformities, observations, or areas for improvement. Non-conformities represent deviations from the requirements of ISO 22301. The auditors will document these findings, categorize them based on severity, and provide you with a clear understanding of the identified issues.

7. Closing Meeting: The external audit concludes with a closing meeting. The auditors will discuss their findings, including any non-conformities or observations, with your organization's representatives. They may provide

preliminary recommendations for corrective actions and improvement opportunities.

8. Audit Report: Following the audit, the certification body will prepare an audit report summarizing the audit findings, including any non-conformities identified. The report may also include recommendations for improvement and suggestions for corrective actions.

9. Corrective Actions: Your organization is responsible for addressing the identified non-conformities and implementing corrective actions. You will develop and implement plans to resolve the non-conformities and improve the BCMS based on the auditors' recommendations.

10. Follow-up Actions: In some cases, the certification body may conduct a follow-up visit or request evidence of corrective actions to verify that the identified non-conformities have been adequately addressed.

11. Certification Decision: The certification body will review the audit report, evidence of corrective actions, and any follow-up activities. Based on their assessment, they will make a decision regarding the issuance of ISO 22301 certification.

It is important to note that the exact steps and duration of the external audit process may vary depending on the certification body, the size and complexity of your organization, and other factors. Communication and collaboration with the certification body are essential throughout the process to ensure a smooth and successful audit.

Key differences between internal and external audits

Internal audits and external audits are both important components of a Business Continuity Management System (BCMS) implementation, but they have distinct differences. Here are the key differences between internal and external audits:

1. Purpose: The primary purpose of internal audits is to assess the effectiveness and compliance of the BCMS within the organization. Internal audits are conducted by internal auditors who are employees of the organization. The focus is on identifying areas for improvement, ensuring adherence to policies and procedures, and verifying compliance with ISO 22301 requirements. On the other hand, the purpose of external audits is to provide an independent and objective assessment of the BCMS. External audits are conducted by auditors from an accredited certification body who are external to the organization. The goal is to validate the compliance of the BCMS with ISO 22301 and provide certification if all requirements are met.

2. Auditors: Internal audits are performed by internal auditors who are employees of the organization. These auditors are familiar with the organization's operations, processes, and systems. External audits are conducted by auditors who are external to the organization and work for an accredited certification body. These auditors bring an impartial perspective and specialized expertise in ISO 22301 requirements.

3. **Reporting Line**: Internal auditors report to the organization's management and are accountable for internal audit findings. They provide feedback directly to the organization to drive improvement. External auditors, on the other hand, report to the certification body and are responsible for assessing compliance with ISO 22301. They issue an audit report that is reviewed by the certification body for certification decisions.

4. **Independence**: Internal auditors are part of the organization and may face challenges related to independence. They must ensure objectivity and impartiality in conducting audits. External auditors, however, are independent of the organization and provide an unbiased assessment of the BCMS. Their independence ensures an impartial evaluation of compliance with ISO 22301.

5. **Frequency**: Internal audits are conducted on a regular basis, as determined by the organization's audit schedule. They may be conducted annually, semi-annually, or as needed. The frequency of internal audits is driven by the organization's internal requirements and the need for ongoing assessment and improvement. External audits, on the other hand, are typically conducted less frequently and are part of the certification process. They occur at specific intervals, such as initial certification audits, surveillance audits, and recertification audits, as determined by the certification body.

6. **Scope**: Internal audits can cover the entire BCMS or focus on specific areas of concern or improvement. The scope of internal audits is flexible and can be adjusted based on the organization's priorities. External audits, however, follow a predefined scope that aligns with the requirements of ISO 22301. The scope of external audits covers the entire BCMS and aims to assess compliance with all relevant ISO 22301 requirements.

While there are differences between internal and external audits, both are essential for the successful implementation and maintenance of a robust BCMS. Internal audits help organizations drive continuous improvement and ensure adherence to their internal policies and procedures. External audits provide independent verification and certification of compliance with ISO 22301, enhancing the organization's credibility and demonstrating their commitment to business continuity.

10.4 ISO 22301 Certification Process

▫Understanding the process of ISO 22301 certification

The process of ISO 22301 certification involves several steps to assess an organization's compliance with the requirements of the standard. Here is an overview of the typical process:

1. **Initial Assessment**: The organization expresses its interest in obtaining ISO 22301 certification and contacts a certification body. The certification body provides information about the certification process, requirements, and costs. The organization evaluates its readiness and decides to proceed with the certification process.

2. Gap Analysis: The organization conducts an internal gap analysis to assess its current state of compliance with the requirements of ISO 22301. This helps identify any gaps or areas of non-compliance that need to be addressed before the formal certification audit.

3. Documentation Review: The organization prepares its BCMS documentation, including policies, procedures, plans, and records, to demonstrate compliance with ISO 22301. The certification body reviews the documentation to ensure it aligns with the standard's requirements.

4. Stage 1 Audit: The certification process typically involves two stages of audits. The Stage 1 audit is a preliminary assessment conducted by the certification body. The auditors evaluate the organization's readiness for the Stage 2 audit. They review the BCMS documentation, assess the implementation status, and identify any major non-conformities that need to be addressed before proceeding to the next stage.

5. Stage 2 Audit: The Stage 2 audit is the main audit where the certification body evaluates the organization's BCMS implementation in depth. The auditors verify the effectiveness and compliance of the BCMS through on-site assessments, interviews, and document reviews. They assess the organization's adherence to ISO 22301 requirements, including risk management, business impact analysis, continuity planning, and testing and exercising activities. The auditors also verify the organization's ability to respond to incidents and recover critical business functions.

6. Non-Conformities and Corrective Actions: During the audit, the auditors may identify non-conformities, observations, or areas for improvement. Non-conformities represent deviations from the requirements of ISO 22301. The organization is responsible for addressing these non-conformities and implementing corrective actions within a specified timeframe. The certification body will review and verify the effectiveness of the corrective actions.

7. Certification Decision: Based on the audit findings and the organization's corrective actions, the certification body makes a certification decision. If the organization has demonstrated compliance with ISO 22301 and has effectively addressed any non-conformities, the certification body issues the ISO 22301 certification.

8. Surveillance Audits: After the initial certification, the organization is subject to periodic surveillance audits by the certification body. These audits ensure that the organization maintains compliance with ISO 22301 over time. Surveillance audits are typically conducted annually or as per the agreed schedule.

9. Recertification: ISO 22301 certification is valid for a specific period, usually three years. Before the certification expires, the organization undergoes a recertification audit to demonstrate its continued compliance with the standard. The recertification process is similar to the initial certification process, including a comprehensive audit of the BCMS.

It is important to note that the exact process and requirements may vary depending on the certification body and the specific circumstances of the organization. Collaboration and communication with the certification body throughout the process are essential to ensure a successful ISO 22301 certification.

Benefits of achieving ISO 22301 certification

Achieving ISO 22301 certification offers numerous benefits for organizations. Here are some key benefits:

1. Enhanced Business Resilience: ISO 22301 certification demonstrates that an organization has implemented a robust and effective Business Continuity Management System (BCMS). It enhances the organization's ability to identify and respond to disruptions, minimize downtime, and quickly recover critical business functions. This resilience strengthens the organization's reputation and instills confidence among stakeholders.

2. Compliance with Best Practices: ISO 22301 is based on international best practices for business continuity management. Achieving certification signifies that an organization complies with these industry-recognized standards. It demonstrates a commitment to following established methodologies and guidelines for identifying, assessing, and managing business continuity risks.

3. Improved Risk Management: ISO 22301 certification helps organizations improve their risk management practices. By conducting a comprehensive business impact analysis (BIA) and risk assessment, organizations gain a deeper understanding of their vulnerabilities and develop strategies to mitigate risks. This proactive approach to risk management enhances the organization's ability to prevent, respond to, and recover from disruptions effectively.

4. Competitive Advantage: ISO 22301 certification provides a competitive advantage in the market. It differentiates an organization from its competitors by showcasing its commitment to maintaining business continuity, even in challenging circumstances. Certification can be a deciding factor for potential customers, partners, and stakeholders who prioritize working with organizations that have demonstrated their resilience and preparedness.

5. Enhanced Reputation and Trust: ISO 22301 certification enhances the organization's reputation and builds trust among customers, clients, suppliers, and other stakeholders. It demonstrates the organization's dedication to maintaining its operations, meeting customer requirements, and ensuring service continuity. Certification instills confidence in stakeholders that the organization can manage disruptions and protect their interests.

6. Regulatory Compliance: ISO 22301 certification helps organizations comply with legal and regulatory requirements related to business continuity management. It ensures that the organization has implemented processes and controls that align with industry regulations, standards, and guidelines. Certification can simplify compliance audits and regulatory assessments, saving time and resources.

7. Effective Communication and Collaboration: ISO 22301 certification promotes effective communication and collaboration within the organization and with external stakeholders. The standardized framework and common language provided by ISO 22301 facilitate clear communication of roles, responsibilities, and procedures during times of disruption. It enhances coordination, cooperation, and alignment among different departments and stakeholders, leading to more efficient and effective business continuity practices.

8. Continuous Improvement: ISO 22301 certification fosters a culture of continuous improvement within the organization. It encourages regular assessment, review, and enhancement of the BCMS to adapt to evolving risks and changing business needs. The certification process itself, including internal and external audits, promotes a systematic approach to identifying areas for improvement and implementing corrective actions.

9. Customer Confidence and Satisfaction: ISO 22301 certification can increase customer confidence and satisfaction. Customers feel reassured knowing that the organization has a well-defined and tested business continuity plan in place. They are more likely to continue doing business with a certified organization, knowing that their needs will be met even during unexpected events.

10. Business Opportunities: ISO 22301 certification opens doors to new business opportunities. Many clients, especially in sectors such as finance, healthcare, and government, require their partners or suppliers to have ISO 22301 certification. Certification can enable organizations to expand their client base, enter new markets, and participate in tenders or contracts that prioritize business continuity management.

Overall, ISO 22301 certification provides tangible benefits in terms of operational resilience, reputation, risk management, and customer confidence. It helps organizations establish a robust business continuity framework and position themselves as reliable and trustworthy partners in the face of disruptions.

10.5 Post-Certification Activities

How to communicate your ISO 22301 certification to stakeholders

Communicating your ISO 22301 certification to stakeholders is crucial to maximize the impact and value of your achievement. Here are some strategies for effectively communicating your ISO 22301 certification:

1. Develop a Communication Plan: Create a comprehensive communication plan that outlines the key messages, target audiences, communication channels, and timelines for sharing the news of your ISO 22301 certification. This plan will help ensure a consistent and coordinated approach to communication.

2. Craft a Press Release: Draft a press release announcing your ISO 22301 certification. Highlight the significance of the certification, its benefits, and what it means for your organization and stakeholders. Distribute the press release to relevant media outlets, industry publications, and online platforms. Leverage your website and social media channels to share the news as well.

3. Internal Communication: Start by communicating the certification internally within your organization. Share the news with employees, management, and key stakeholders through internal newsletters, emails, intranet updates, or dedicated staff meetings. Emphasize the importance of the certification and its relevance to the organization's commitment to business continuity and resilience.

4. External Communication: Reach out to your external stakeholders, such as customers, clients, suppliers, partners, and industry associations, to inform them about your ISO 22301 certification. Utilize various channels like email newsletters, client communication platforms, supplier portals, and industry events to share the news. Highlight how the certification enhances your ability to provide uninterrupted services and meet their business continuity requirements.

5. Website and Marketing Collateral: Update your organization's website to prominently feature the ISO 22301 certification logo and a dedicated section highlighting the significance of the certification. Incorporate the certification logo in your marketing collateral, including brochures, presentations, and business cards. This will visually communicate your commitment to business continuity to anyone interacting with your organization.

6. Case Studies and Success Stories: Develop case studies or success stories that showcase how your organization's implementation of ISO 22301 has positively impacted your business continuity and resilience. Highlight specific challenges faced, solutions implemented, and measurable results achieved. Share these case studies with stakeholders to demonstrate the practical application and value of ISO 22301 certification.

7. Engage with Industry Networks: Participate in industry conferences, seminars, and networking events related to business continuity and resilience. Use these opportunities to share your ISO 22301 certification journey, lessons learned, and best practices with peers and industry experts. Consider speaking at relevant events or hosting webinars to share insights and experiences.

8. Customer Communication: Proactively communicate your ISO 22301 certification to existing and potential customers. Include information about the certification in your proposals, sales pitches, and customer meetings. Emphasize how the certification demonstrates your commitment to their business continuity needs and assures them of your resilience in the face of disruptions.

9. Continuous Communication: Certification is an ongoing commitment. Continuously communicate the importance of ISO 22301 and your dedication to maintaining and improving your business continuity practices. Provide regular updates on your BCMS initiatives, key milestones, and any further improvements or achievements related to ISO 22301.

10. Feedback and Engagement: Encourage feedback and engagement from stakeholders regarding your ISO 22301 certification. Actively listen to their perspectives, address any concerns or queries, and showcase how their input

has influenced your business continuity strategies. This demonstrates transparency, responsiveness, and a commitment to continuous improvement.

Remember, effective communication is key to maximizing the impact of your ISO 22301 certification. Tailor your communication efforts to the specific needs and expectations of your stakeholders, keeping them informed, engaged, and confident in your organization's ability to manage disruptions and maintain business continuity.

Maintaining your ISO 22301 certification

Maintaining your ISO 22301 certification requires ongoing commitment and effort to ensure the continued effectiveness and compliance of your Business Continuity Management System (BCMS). Here are some key steps to help you maintain your ISO 22301 certification:

1. Continual Improvement: Embrace a culture of continual improvement within your organization. Regularly review and assess your BCMS to identify areas for enhancement. Encourage feedback from stakeholders and employees to gather insights for improvement opportunities. Implement corrective actions to address any non-conformities or areas of improvement identified during audits or reviews.

2. Compliance Monitoring: Maintain a proactive approach to monitoring and ensuring compliance with ISO 22301 requirements. Regularly review your BCMS documentation, procedures, and processes to ensure they remain up to date and aligned with the standard. Conduct internal audits at planned intervals to assess compliance and identify any gaps or non-conformities.

3. Internal Audits: Conduct regular internal audits of your BCMS to evaluate its effectiveness and identify areas for improvement. Ensure that your internal audit program covers all relevant areas of the standard and includes a robust assessment of your BCMS processes, controls, and performance indicators. Use the findings from internal audits to drive continual improvement efforts.

4. Management Reviews: Conduct periodic management reviews of your BCMS to evaluate its ongoing suitability, adequacy, and effectiveness. Involve top management in the review process to ensure their commitment and support. Assess the performance of your BCMS against defined objectives, key performance indicators, and relevant benchmarks. Use the outcomes of the management reviews to identify areas for improvement and set goals for the next period.

5. Training and Awareness: Maintain a comprehensive training and awareness program to ensure that employees at all levels of the organization understand their roles and responsibilities in implementing and maintaining the BCMS. Regularly provide training sessions, workshops, and refresher courses to enhance competence and keep employees informed about changes or updates to the BCMS.

6. Documentation Control: Ensure proper control and management of your BCMS documentation. Regularly review and update your policies, procedures, plans, and records to reflect any changes in your organization's processes or

business environment. Keep a documented history of changes and ensure that all employees have access to the most up-to-date versions of relevant documentation.

7. External Surveillance Audits: Cooperate with the certification body for scheduled surveillance audits. These audits are conducted by the certification body at planned intervals to assess the ongoing compliance and effectiveness of your BCMS. Address any non-conformities identified during these audits and implement appropriate corrective actions within the specified timeframes.

8. Continuous Communication: Communicate your commitment to maintaining ISO 22301 certification to your stakeholders, including customers, clients, suppliers, and employees. Provide regular updates on your BCMS performance, improvements, and achievements. Engage with stakeholders to gather feedback and demonstrate your responsiveness to their needs.

9. Review and Update Risk Assessments: Regularly review and update your risk assessments and business impact analyses to reflect changes in your business environment, operations, or organizational structure. Ensure that your risk assessments cover potential disruptions and their potential impacts on your critical business functions.

10. External Changes: Stay informed about external changes, such as updates to ISO 22301 or relevant industry regulations and incorporate them into your BCMS. Continuously monitor changes in your business environment, technology landscape, and stakeholder expectations to adapt your BCMS accordingly.

By following these steps and maintaining a proactive approach to BCMS management, you can ensure the ongoing effectiveness, compliance, and value of your ISO 22301 certification. Regular assessments, audits, and improvement initiatives will help you strengthen your business continuity capabilities and maintain stakeholder confidence in your organization's ability to manage disruptions.

10.6 Surveillance and Recertification Audits

Surveillance and recertification audits play a crucial role in maintaining ISO 22301 certification and demonstrating the ongoing compliance and effectiveness of your Business Continuity Management System (BCMS). Let's explore the significance and process of surveillance and recertification audits:

Surveillance Audits:

1. Purpose: Surveillance audits are periodic assessments conducted by the certification body to monitor the continued compliance and effectiveness of your BCMS. They verify that your organization maintains the requirements of ISO 22301 between recertification audits.

2. Frequency: Surveillance audits are typically conducted annually or as per the certification body's defined schedule. The frequency may vary depending on factors such as the maturity of your BCMS, risk factors, and certification body requirements.

3. Scope: The scope of surveillance audits generally focuses on key elements of the BCMS, including the implementation of controls, performance measurement, management commitment, and continuous improvement efforts. The auditors will select specific areas to assess based on risk and previous audit findings.

4. Process: Surveillance audits follow a similar process to initial certification audits, involving document reviews, interviews, and observations of BCMS practices. The auditors assess the ongoing conformity of your BCMS with ISO 22301 requirements, identify areas for improvement, and review actions taken since the previous audit.

5. Findings and Non-Conformities: The audit findings, including any identified non-conformities or opportunities for improvement, are documented in an audit report. Non-conformities require corrective actions within a specified timeframe to address deviations from ISO 22301 requirements.

Recertification Audits:

1. Purpose: Recertification audits are comprehensive assessments conducted to renew your ISO 22301 certification. They validate the continued compliance and effectiveness of your BCMS, taking into account changes within your organization and the external business environment since the previous certification.

2. Frequency: Recertification audits typically occur every three years, although the exact timeframe may depend on certification body requirements. They are more extensive than surveillance audits and involve a thorough review of your entire BCMS.

3. Process: Recertification audits encompass document reviews, interviews, observations, and a comprehensive assessment of your BCMS. The auditors evaluate the effectiveness of your BCMS in achieving desired outcomes, assess the extent of compliance with ISO 22301 requirements, and identify areas for improvement.

4. Findings and Non-Conformities: Similar to surveillance audits, the findings and non-conformities identified during recertification audits are documented in an audit report. Non-conformities must be addressed within a specified timeframe to maintain or renew your ISO 22301 certification.

5. Certification Decision: Based on the audit findings, corrective actions, and compliance with ISO 22301 requirements, the certification body will make a decision regarding the continuation or renewal of your ISO 22301 certification.

It is essential to engage proactively with surveillance and recertification audits, ensuring that your BCMS remains robust and aligned with ISO 22301 requirements. Address any non-conformities identified, implement necessary corrective actions, and leverage the audit findings to drive continual improvement in your organization's business continuity capabilities. These audits provide assurance to stakeholders that your organization remains committed to maintaining effective business continuity management.

The necessity and process of surveillance audits

Surveillance audits are an essential part of maintaining ISO 22301 certification. These audits are conducted by the certification body at regular intervals, typically once a year, to assess the ongoing compliance and effectiveness of your Business Continuity Management System (BCMS). Here's an overview of the necessity and process of surveillance audits:

Necessity of Surveillance Audits:

1. Verify Ongoing Compliance: Surveillance audits ensure that your organization continues to comply with the requirements of ISO 22301. They validate that your BCMS remains effective and aligned with the standard, demonstrating your commitment to maintaining business continuity.

2. Assess Performance and Improvement: Surveillance audits assess the performance of your BCMS and its ability to achieve the desired outcomes. They help identify areas for improvement, address any non-conformities, and measure the effectiveness of corrective actions taken based on previous audit findings.

3. Maintain Certification Validity: Surveillance audits are necessary to maintain the validity of your ISO 22301 certification. Failure to participate in surveillance audits or address non-conformities identified during the audits can result in the suspension or withdrawal of your certification.

Process of Surveillance Audits:

1. Audit Planning: The certification body will inform you in advance about the schedule and scope of the surveillance audit. They will provide specific details regarding the auditors' visit, duration of the audit, and any documentation or information they require.

2. Document Review: The auditors will review your BCMS documentation, including policies, procedures, plans, and records, to ensure they are up to date and aligned with ISO 22301 requirements. They may request additional documentation or information to verify compliance.

3. On-Site Assessment: The auditors will conduct an on-site assessment of your BCMS. They will interview personnel, observe processes, and review evidence of implementation to evaluate the effectiveness of your BCMS in practice. The auditors will also assess your organization's response capabilities and the integration of business continuity principles into your daily operations.

4. Non-Conformity Identification: If any non-conformities or areas for improvement are identified during the surveillance audit, the auditors will document them. Non-conformities represent deviations from ISO 22301 requirements, and they need to be addressed within a specified timeframe.

5. Corrective Actions: Based on the audit findings, you will be required to implement corrective actions to address any identified non-conformities. The auditors will review the effectiveness of these corrective actions during subsequent surveillance audits.

6. Audit Report: The auditors will prepare an audit report that includes their findings, recommendations, and any non-conformities identified. The report will also highlight the positive aspects of your BCMS and commendable practices.

7. Follow-up Actions: If non-conformities were identified, you must implement corrective actions within the specified timeframe. The certification body may conduct a follow-up assessment to verify the effectiveness of these actions.

8. Certification Decision: Based on the audit findings, corrective actions, and compliance with ISO 22301 requirements, the certification body will make a decision regarding the continuation of your ISO 22301 certification.

Remember that surveillance audits are an opportunity to continually improve your BCMS and demonstrate your commitment to maintaining business continuity. Actively participate in the audit process, address any non-conformities, and use the findings to drive ongoing improvement in your organization's business continuity capabilities.

Understanding recertification audits

Recertification audits play a vital role in the ongoing maintenance of your ISO 22301 certification. These audits are conducted periodically to assess the continued compliance and effectiveness of your Business Continuity Management System (BCMS). Here is a closer look at recertification audits:

Purpose of Recertification Audits: Recertification audits are performed to verify that your organization's BCMS continues to meet the requirements of ISO 22301. The goal is to assess the maturity and effectiveness of your BCMS and ensure its alignment with the standard. Recertification audits provide an opportunity to demonstrate your commitment to business continuity and validate the ongoing effectiveness of your BCMS.

Timing of Recertification Audits: Recertification audits typically occur every three years, although the specific timing may vary depending on certification body requirements. The purpose is to provide a comprehensive evaluation of your BCMS over a defined period, ensuring that your certification remains valid and up to date.

Process of Recertification Audits: The process of a recertification audit is similar to that of an initial certification audit but with a focus on assessing the continued compliance and effectiveness of your BCMS. The audit involves several steps:

1. Pre-Audit Preparation: Before the recertification audit, you should review and update your BCMS documentation, processes, and procedures to ensure they reflect any changes within your organization. This includes addressing any non-conformities identified in previous audits and implementing necessary corrective actions.

2. Audit Planning: The certification body will work with you to schedule the recertification audit and outline the audit scope and objectives. This includes determining the areas to be audited, the timeline, and the resources required.

3. Document Review: The auditors will review your BCMS documentation, including policies, procedures, plans, and records, to assess their alignment with ISO 22301 requirements. They will also examine evidence of the implementation and effectiveness of your BCMS.

4. On-Site Assessment: The auditors will conduct on-site visits to evaluate the practical implementation of your BCMS. They will interview employees, observe processes, and assess the effectiveness of controls and risk management practices.

5. Non-Conformities and Corrective Actions: If any non-conformities are identified during the recertification audit, they will be documented in an audit report. You will be required to address these non-conformities within a specified timeframe and provide evidence of the corrective actions taken.

6. Certification Decision: Based on the findings of the recertification audit and the effectiveness of your corrective actions, the certification body will make a decision regarding the renewal of your ISO 22301 certification. If all requirements are met, your certification will be renewed for another defined period.

It is crucial to approach recertification audits with the same level of preparation and commitment as initial certification audits. Continuously monitor and improve your BCMS, address any non-conformities promptly, and ensure the ongoing effectiveness of your business continuity practices. Recertification audits provide an opportunity to validate the continued relevance and compliance of your BCMS, instilling confidence in your organization's ability to manage disruptions and maintain business continuity.

10.7 Managing Non-Conformities During External Audits

▫Handling non-conformities identified during an external audit

Handling non-conformities identified during an external audit is an essential part of maintaining ISO 22301 compliance and ensuring the effectiveness of your Business Continuity Management System (BCMS). Here are some key steps to effectively address non-conformities:

1. Understand the Non-Conformity: Thoroughly review the non-conformity identified in the audit report. Understand the specific requirement of ISO 22301 that was not met and the reasons behind it. Analyze the impact of the non-conformity on your BCMS and the potential risks associated with it.

2. Investigate the Root Cause: Conduct a root cause analysis to identify the underlying reasons for the non-conformity. Determine whether the non-conformity was caused by a breakdown in processes, inadequate resources, lack of training, or any other factors. This analysis will help you address the core issue and prevent similar non-conformities in the future.

3. Develop Corrective Actions: Develop a detailed corrective action plan to address the non-conformity effectively. Define specific actions to rectify the identified issues, improve processes, and ensure compliance with the relevant

ISO 22301 requirement. Assign responsibilities, set realistic timelines, and establish clear success criteria for each corrective action.

4. Implement Corrective Actions: Put the corrective actions into practice within the defined timeframe. Ensure that all necessary resources, including personnel, training, and documentation, are made available to support the implementation. Monitor the progress of each corrective action and document the steps taken to address the non-conformity.

5. Verify Effectiveness: Once the corrective actions have been implemented, conduct an internal review or self-assessment to verify their effectiveness. This may involve conducting tests, audits, or other evaluations to ensure that the non-conformity has been adequately addressed and the BCMS is now in compliance with ISO 22301.

6. Document the Process: Maintain clear documentation of the non-conformity, the root cause analysis, the corrective actions taken, and the verification of their effectiveness. These records serve as evidence of your commitment to addressing non-conformities and maintaining an effective BCMS.

7. Communicate with the Certification Body: Keep the certification body informed about the non-conformity and your corrective actions. Provide them with the necessary documentation and evidence to demonstrate that the non-conformity has been appropriately addressed. Cooperate with any follow-up assessments or requests from the certification body to verify the effectiveness of the corrective actions.

8. Continuous Improvement: Use the experience of addressing non-conformities as an opportunity for improvement. Learn from the non-conformities and take steps to prevent their recurrence. Review your BCMS processes, update policies or procedures if necessary, and provide additional training or resources to enhance compliance with ISO 22301 requirements.

By promptly addressing non-conformities and implementing effective corrective actions, you demonstrate your commitment to maintaining a robust and compliant BCMS. This proactive approach not only ensures ISO 22301 compliance but also strengthens your organization's resilience and ability to manage disruptions effectively.

Developing and implementing a corrective action plan

Developing and implementing a corrective action plan is crucial when addressing non-conformities identified during an external audit. Here are the key steps to develop and implement an effective corrective action plan:

1. Identify the Non-Conformity: Thoroughly review the audit findings and identify the specific non-conformity that needs to be addressed. Clearly define the deviation from the ISO 22301 requirements and understand its impact on your BCMS.

2. Conduct Root Cause Analysis: Perform a root cause analysis to determine the underlying factors that led to the non-conformity. Identify the root cause by

asking "why" multiple times to get to the core issue. This analysis helps uncover the underlying systemic or process-related issues that need to be addressed.

3. Set Clear Objectives: Clearly define the objectives of the corrective action plan. State what needs to be achieved and the desired outcome. The objectives should be specific, measurable, achievable, relevant, and time-bound (SMART).

4. Develop Corrective Actions: Based on the identified root cause, develop specific corrective actions that will address the non-conformity. Each corrective action should be clear, actionable, and focused on preventing the recurrence of the non-conformity. Assign responsibilities to individuals or teams who will be responsible for implementing the corrective actions.

5. Determine Resources and Timeline: Identify the necessary resources, such as personnel, training, technology, or financial resources, required to implement the corrective actions. Define a realistic timeline for each action, considering the complexity and urgency of the non-conformity.

6. Implementation and Monitoring: Put the corrective actions into practice. Monitor the progress and ensure that each action is being implemented according to the defined timeline. Regularly communicate with the responsible individuals or teams, provide necessary support, and address any obstacles that may arise during implementation.

7. Measure Effectiveness: Define appropriate metrics or key performance indicators (KPIs) to measure the effectiveness of the corrective actions. Monitor and collect data to assess whether the corrective actions are achieving the desired outcomes and addressing the non-conformity. Analyze the data to ensure the actions have been successful.

8. Review and Verification: Conduct a review or verification process to evaluate the effectiveness of the corrective actions. This may involve conducting internal audits, self-assessments, or seeking input from relevant stakeholders. Verify that the non-conformity has been fully addressed and that the BCMS is now in compliance with ISO 22301 requirements.

9. Documentation and Communication: Document all aspects of the corrective action plan, including the identified non-conformity, root cause analysis, corrective actions taken, resources utilized, timelines, and verification results. Communicate the progress and outcomes to relevant stakeholders, including the certification body if required.

10. Continual Improvement: Use the corrective action process as an opportunity for continual improvement. Learn from the non-conformity and identify areas where the BCMS can be strengthened. Update policies, procedures, or training programs to prevent similar non-conformities in the future.

Remember, the corrective action plan should be comprehensive, well-documented, and result oriented. It should address the root cause of the non-conformity and ensure that the BCMS is brought back into compliance with ISO 22301 requirements.

Regularly monitor and review the effectiveness of the corrective actions to maintain a robust and continually improving BCMS.

10.8 Leveraging ISO 22301 Certification for Business Advantage

How to utilize ISO 22301 certification for enhancing business reputation

Utilizing ISO 22301 certification can significantly enhance your business reputation and demonstrate your commitment to effective business continuity management. Here are some key strategies to leverage ISO 22301 certification for enhancing your business reputation:

1. Communicate the Certification: Prominently communicate your ISO 22301 certification to stakeholders, including customers, partners, suppliers, and employees. Display the certification logo on your website, marketing materials, and company documents to showcase your commitment to business continuity and resilience.

2. Highlight the Benefits: Emphasize the benefits of ISO 22301 certification to your stakeholders. Communicate how it demonstrates your ability to effectively manage disruptions, minimize downtime, and safeguard critical operations. Showcase how the certification helps protect stakeholders' interests and ensures the continuity of your products or services.

3. Incorporate it in Proposals and Bids: Include your ISO 22301 certification as a credential in business proposals and bids. Highlight how the certification provides a competitive advantage, ensures business continuity, and enhances risk management. It can strengthen your position and instill confidence in potential customers and partners.

4. Share Success Stories: Share success stories and case studies that illustrate how ISO 22301 certification has helped your organization navigate disruptions and maintain operations. Highlight specific incidents or situations where your business continuity capabilities were put to the test and how ISO 22301 played a vital role in ensuring resilience and successful recovery.

5. Engage in Thought Leadership: Position your organization as a thought leader in business continuity management. Share insights, best practices, and industry trends through articles, blog posts, whitepapers, or speaking engagements. Demonstrate your expertise in implementing ISO 22301 and how it contributes to overall business resilience.

6. Collaborate with Certified Partners: Strengthen your reputation by partnering with other ISO 22301 certified organizations. Collaborate on joint initiatives, events, or projects to showcase a collective commitment to business continuity and leverage each other's expertise.

7. Continuous Improvement: Maintain a focus on continuous improvement of your BCMS. Regularly review and update your processes, procedures, and

strategies to enhance the effectiveness of your business continuity practices. Communicate your dedication to ongoing improvement and highlight how it aligns with ISO 22301 principles.

8. Seek Customer Feedback: Gather feedback from your customers regarding their perception of your business continuity capabilities and the value they derive from your ISO 22301 certification. Use this feedback to understand their needs better, address any concerns, and demonstrate your commitment to meeting their expectations.

9. Engage Employees: Involve your employees in promoting and maintaining the ISO 22301 certification. Ensure they understand the significance of the certification, their role in supporting business continuity, and how it contributes to the organization's reputation. Foster a culture of awareness and accountability throughout the organization.

10. Regularly Monitor and Evaluate: Continuously monitor and evaluate the effectiveness of your BCMS and its alignment with ISO 22301 requirements. Regularly assess customer satisfaction, internal audits, and performance metrics to identify areas for improvement and demonstrate your commitment to maintaining a high standard of business continuity management.

By leveraging ISO 22301 certification and effectively communicating its value, you can enhance your business reputation as a reliable and resilient organization. This can instill trust, attract customers, foster partnerships, and differentiate you from competitors in the market.

The impact of ISO 22301 certification on business resilience and growth

ISO 22301 certification can have a significant impact on business resilience and growth. Here are some keyways in which ISO 22301 certification can positively influence your organization:

1. Enhanced Business Resilience: ISO 22301 certification demonstrates your organization's commitment to business continuity management. By implementing the standard's requirements, you establish robust processes and procedures to identify and mitigate risks, manage disruptions, and ensure the continuity of critical operations. This enables your organization to effectively respond to and recover from incidents, minimizing downtime and financial losses. The certification helps strengthen your overall business resilience, enabling you to withstand disruptions and maintain operations, which in turn safeguards your reputation and customer trust.

2. Improved Risk Management: ISO 22301 certification requires a thorough risk assessment and business impact analysis process. By identifying potential risks and their impacts on your organization, you can proactively implement risk mitigation strategies. This leads to improved risk management practices, helping you identify and address vulnerabilities in your operations and supply chain. The systematic approach mandated by ISO 22301 ensures that risks are regularly reviewed and mitigated, reducing the likelihood of incidents and their potential impact on your organization's growth.

3. **Competitive Advantage**: ISO 22301 certification provides a competitive edge in the market. It demonstrates to customers, partners, and stakeholders that your organization is dedicated to maintaining uninterrupted operations and ensuring the delivery of products or services even in challenging circumstances. The certification can differentiate you from competitors who may not have the same level of business continuity management in place. This competitive advantage can help attract new customers, secure partnerships, and enhance your reputation in the industry, leading to business growth.

4. **Customer Confidence and Trust**: ISO 22301 certification enhances customer confidence and trust in your organization. Customers value suppliers and service providers who can demonstrate their ability to manage disruptions effectively and ensure the continuity of critical services. The certification provides assurance that your organization has implemented internationally recognized best practices in business continuity management. It gives customers peace of mind, knowing that their interests will be safeguarded, and their needs will be met even during challenging times.

5. **Regulatory Compliance**: ISO 22301 certification ensures that your organization meets regulatory requirements related to business continuity and disaster recovery. It helps you align your practices with industry-specific regulations and guidelines, ensuring compliance with legal and regulatory obligations. This can mitigate the risk of penalties, legal issues, and reputational damage associated with non-compliance. Compliance with ISO 22301 requirements positions your organization as a responsible and trustworthy entity in the eyes of regulators, fostering a positive relationship and reducing regulatory risks.

6. **Continuous Improvement Culture**: ISO 22301 certification promotes a culture of continuous improvement within your organization. The standard requires regular monitoring, evaluation, and refinement of your business continuity management system. This focus on continuous improvement fosters a proactive mindset, encouraging employees to identify opportunities for enhancement, innovate, and adapt to changing circumstances. A culture of continuous improvement strengthens your organization's ability to navigate challenges, capitalize on opportunities, and drive sustainable growth.

In summary, ISO 22301 certification positively impacts business resilience and growth by establishing effective business continuity management practices, improving risk management, providing a competitive advantage, instilling customer confidence, ensuring regulatory compliance, and fostering a culture of continuous improvement. The certification demonstrates your commitment to delivering uninterrupted services, protecting stakeholders' interests, and positioning your organization as a reliable and resilient partner in the market.

10.9 Summary

▫ Recap of the external audit process and the journey to ISO 22301 certification

In summary, the external audit process and the journey to ISO 22301 certification involve several key steps and considerations. Here's a recap of the process:

1. Preparation: Prepare your organization for an external audit by ensuring that your BCMS is fully implemented, documented, and aligned with the requirements of ISO 22301. Conduct internal audits and self-assessments to identify any gaps or areas for improvement.

2. Selecting a Certification Body: Choose a credible certification body that has the necessary expertise and accreditation to perform the ISO 22301 certification audit. Consider their experience, reputation, and industry recognition.

3. External Audit Process: The external audit process involves an assessment of your BCMS by the certification body's auditors. They will review your documentation, interview personnel, and observe processes to verify compliance with ISO 22301 requirements.

4. Handling Non-Conformities: If any non-conformities are identified during the audit, take prompt action to address them. Develop a corrective action plan, implement the necessary changes, and verify their effectiveness.

5. Certification Decision: Based on the audit findings, the certification body will make a certification decision. If your organization has successfully met all the requirements of ISO 22301, you will receive the certification.

6. Utilizing ISO 22301 Certification: Leverage your ISO 22301 certification to enhance your business reputation. Communicate the certification to stakeholders, highlight the benefits, incorporate it into proposals and bids, and share success stories.

7. Maintaining Certification: Once certified, continue to maintain and improve your BCMS. Regularly monitor and evaluate its effectiveness, conduct internal audits, and participate in surveillance audits by the certification body to ensure ongoing compliance with ISO 22301.

8. Recertification Audits: Recertification audits are conducted periodically to renew your ISO 22301 certification. These audits assess the continued compliance and effectiveness of your BCMS.

The journey to ISO 22301 certification is a continuous process of improving your business continuity management practices, fostering resilience, and demonstrating your commitment to stakeholders. It involves proactive planning, implementation, and ongoing monitoring and improvement of your BCMS. By achieving ISO 22301 certification, you position your organization as a reliable and resilient entity, capable of managing disruptions and ensuring business continuity.

Remember that ISO 22301 certification is not an endpoint but a milestone in your organization's journey towards effective business continuity management. Continual improvement, ongoing maintenance, and a commitment to best practices are essential for maximizing the benefits of ISO 22301 certification and ensuring long-term success in managing business disruptions.

Looking beyond certification: fostering a culture of business continuity and resilience

Looking beyond certification, fostering a culture of business continuity and resilience is essential for long-term success in managing disruptions. Here are key considerations to cultivate such a culture:

1. Leadership Commitment: Leaders should actively demonstrate their commitment to business continuity and resilience. They should communicate the importance of these practices, provide necessary resources, and lead by example. Their visible commitment fosters a culture where business continuity becomes ingrained in the organization's values.

2. Employee Engagement: Engage employees at all levels in the development and implementation of business continuity practices. Encourage their involvement in risk assessments, incident response planning, and recovery exercises. Create channels for them to provide feedback, share ideas, and contribute to the ongoing improvement of the BCMS.

3. Awareness and Training: Promote awareness and provide training on business continuity and resilience. Regularly communicate the importance of these practices, educate employees on their roles and responsibilities, and provide training on incident response procedures. This helps build a shared understanding and competence throughout the organization.

4. Continuous Improvement: Foster a culture of continuous improvement where learning from incidents and near-misses is encouraged. Regularly review and update business continuity plans, procedures, and strategies based on lessons learned. Encourage employees to propose improvements and implement changes that enhance the organization's resilience.

5. Integration with Business Processes: Integrate business continuity and resilience considerations into day-to-day operations and decision-making processes. Incorporate business continuity requirements into project management methodologies, procurement processes, and business planning activities. This ensures that resilience becomes an integral part of the organization's overall operations.

6. Testing and Exercises: Regularly conduct testing and exercises to validate the effectiveness of your business continuity plans. Simulate various scenarios and evaluate the response and recovery capabilities of the organization. This not only identifies areas for improvement but also builds confidence and familiarity with the BCMS among employees.

7. Sharing Best Practices: Encourage the sharing of best practices and lessons learned both internally and externally. Participate in industry forums, collaborate with peers, and share success stories to inspire others. By sharing experiences and knowledge, you contribute to the collective resilience of the broader business community.

8. Continual Communication: Maintain open and transparent communication channels related to business continuity and resilience. Regularly update

employees on the organization's BCMS activities, progress, and achievements. Provide information on emerging risks, changes in procedures, and lessons learned from incidents. Effective communication builds trust and ensures everyone is well-informed and prepared.

9. Performance Measurement: Establish key performance indicators (KPIs) and metrics to monitor the effectiveness of your BCMS. Regularly measure and report on these metrics to assess the organization's resilience and identify areas for improvement. Use this data to drive decision-making and prioritize resources for further enhancement.

10. Review and Adaptation: Continuously review and adapt your BCMS to evolving threats, regulatory requirements, and business changes. Regularly conduct management reviews, engage in risk assessments, and stay updated on emerging trends in business continuity management. This enables your organization to proactively address new challenges and maintain a state of readiness.

By fostering a culture of business continuity and resilience, organizations go beyond certification to embed these practices into their DNA. This culture ensures that business continuity becomes a shared responsibility, ingrained in everyday operations, and responsive to evolving risks. It positions the organization for long-term success in managing disruptions and maintaining operational continuity.

In this final chapter, the readers will gain insights into the certification process and learn practical tips on maintaining their certification, dealing with non-conformities, and leveraging their ISO 22301 certification for business advantage. Real-life case studies and examples will be provided for better understanding.

Made in the USA
Coppell, TX
28 June 2024